# Beyond Demographics the Truth about Diversity

GARY RICHARDSON

GARY RICHARDSON

Copyright © 2017 Gary Richardson

All rights reserved.

ISBN-10:0999500503

ISBN-13:978-0999500507

# BEYOND DEMOGRAPHICS

GARY RICHARDSON

# DEDICATION

This book is dedicated to my loving parents Johnnie and Mattie Richardson. I can never repay you for the love you have given me throughout my life. I hope I have made you proud as your son

# BEYOND DEMOGRAPHICS

GARY RICHARDSON

# CONTENTS

|  | Acknowledgments | I |
|---|---|---|
|  | Introduction | Pg 8 |
| 1 | Destination Diversity | Pg 18 |
| 2 | Laying the Foundation | Pg 28 |
| 3 | Exposing the Barriers | Pg 42 |
| 4 | Comprehending the Concept of Diversity | Pg 60 |
| 5 | Personal Contribution | Pg 76 |
| 6 | Preparation is Tougher than the Game | Pg 86 |
| 7 | Putting Things in Order | Pg 112 |
| 8 | The Recipe | Pg 133 |
| 9 | How Diversity Shaped my Careers | Pg 152 |

## ACKNOWLEDGMENTS

I would like to say thank you to my loving parents, Johnnie and Mattie Richardson for bringing me into the world and raising me to believe in God and trusting my abilities. To my wife Sheila for being my cheerleader and supporting me throughout this project. To my children, Edward, Sheena, Ebony, Ajia, Xavier, and Julius for giving me a reason to leave a legacy. To my brothers Ernest, Andre, Johnnie, and sister DeAnn for being my heroes throughout my life and always encouraging me to be my best. To (Ret.) Lt. Col. Mark Brady for being the one responsible for helping me find my purpose in life as a diversity practitioner. To Dr. Judith Mathewson for being my greatest mentor and career development angel. To Mr. Nathan Thomas for your marches alongside Dr. Martin Luther King Jr. in the fight for equality and being there when I needed you. To Jerome John for being my right hand, friend, and guardian angel during my time with the New York State Police. To Elliot Boyce for looking out for me when you didn't have to and speaking on my behalf. To Marco Rahn for being my true friend and brother. To Charles Underwood for being my confidant and brother. Finally, to Nancy Riesbeck for igniting the fire in me to put my experiences on paper. Thank you all for traveling on this journey with me.

## Introduction

"What! Not another damn diversity class. We don't need this sensitivity bullshit! Minorities need to stop complaining and just work harder!" Imagine walking into a classroom to give a lecture on diversity, and this is the first thing you hear. These are harsh words for even the most seasoned speakers to hear, but when training is forced down people's throats and the subject itself hasn't been properly framed; statements like this are the result.

Over the last seventeen years, I have dedicated my life to teaching the concept of diversity. I was compelled to write this book to capture the events, which led to my breakthrough in understanding that the concept of diversity is more than simply the "right thing to do" or a "politically correct gesture of kindness." My journey is as much a story about discovery as it is about gaining an appreciation for empathy. I want to give people the opportunity to experience diversity without forcing its purpose into a neat little box of academic terms and statistics. When described that way, it loses any personal connection.

I've witnessed first-hand the frustration and anger from workers who suffer from "diversity fatigue" because they're forced to listen, over and over again, to a process which doesn't seem to have any face value for White males or the generation X,Y, or Z's who don't think it's necessary. They latter groups were born into a world without some of the racial lines of demarcation, like Baby Boomers and Millennials. Some of their best friends really *are* black! It's not just a politically correct statement for younger generations.

Others feel that after decades of research and millions of dollars spent on training, diversity hasn't done much to advance women and minorities in the workplace. This criticism is accurate when you analyze the number of women and minority CEOs of Fortune 500 companies or those who hold senior leadership positions within our military branches. Currently, there are twenty- three women (4.6%) holding CEO positions in the Fortune 500 companies: extremely low, considering that women make up just over fifty-one percent of our population. Blacks hold much lower numbers of the top CEO positions, with a total of four breaking the glass ceiling. Not four percent, folks: just four - the number that follows three. As a whole, minorities make up only four percent of top CEOs, which includes blacks, Asians, and Latin Americans.

The United States Military has similar shortages at its most senior levels of leadership. At the General ranks, women and minorities make up less than one percent across all branches of service. That's important because this is the level at which policies are created which affect a diverse group of members and civilian employees. I will stop with number counting now because I believe that this is what's leading organizations down the wrong path. We relied entirely too much on numbers to determine diversity's success or failure in the workplace.

This may sound crazy, coming from a black man, but diversity is not black, White, sexual orientation, gender, race, color, religion, or any other demographic category we've created for ourselves. Diversity is an active process that cannot be measured simply by counting the number of women and minorities in an organization. I know this because I've been both beneficiary and victim of this type of thinking. I've been selected for a job based on the fact that the organization needed more minorities. However, once employed, I wasn't completely accepted as a full-fledged member of the team. As grateful as I was to be employed, in no way did my hiring create diversity? The thought still exists that if we collect a comfortable number of people who aren't White, male, and heterosexual, we'd have diversity!

This is a completely flawed ideology. Hiring people simply because they're underrepresented in the workplace isn't an automatic default for success. How does this approach relate to increased profits, mission readiness, or goal accomplishments? It doesn't - people of different colors, races, or religious beliefs, all corralled together under one roof is being diverse. You can *be* diverse, but you can't have diversity. You must *have* diversity, and it takes work to achieve it. This is also why I never use the term "diversity and inclusion." True diversity *is* inclusive; otherwise, you just have an eclectic group of people.

Not many people seem to understand the concept beyond demographic categories such as race, color, gender, etc. To the contrary, most of what contributes to diversity lies beneath the surface of a person's skin and is only revealed under the right conditions. Creative thinking, ingenuity, and judgment, for example, are characteristics that aren't exposed until we're faced with a problem or goal to accomplish. Picture it this way: if you have a cell phone, I'm sure you know it's capable of receiving and making outgoing calls, reading, receiving and sending texts and emails; but what else can it do? If I asked you how many apps your phone has and how they perform, could you tell me without flipping through the screens or going back to the instruction manual? I'm going to guess, probably not. This means you're not using your phone to its full potential.

Not being able to answer these questions doesn't remove these apps from your phone; nor does it stop them from running and burning up your battery. They're sitting there, ready to be used. Some of them can save both time and money, or at least help you reserve a table at one of the best restaurants in town. The key is tapping into the apps and learning what they can do and how to make them perform. The concept of diversity works the same way. Characteristics such as artistic talent, the ability to reason, sound judgment, and creative problem-solving skills aren't seen. They are programmed and developed within us, waiting to be discovered; waiting to be used. The users (organizations) must find the apps we all possess inside and enable employees to use them, to become more productive. This is what workplace diversity is about.

I'd love to claim that I was a child prodigy and came out of the womb knowing all there is to know on the subject, but that isn't the case. It took me some twenty years and a lot of work and life experience before I understood the concept for what it truly represents. I know the journey has made me a better person, a better consultant, and a better diversity practitioner because I speak from hands-on experience; not theory. What I've learned didn't come from books - it came from lessons learned through my own struggles in life and my professional careers. In my opinion, diversity must be experienced in order to know how to apply it effectively.

I've experienced diversity firsthand as a New York State Trooper working side by side with New York City firefighters and the NYPD during the horrific events of 9/11.

I remember driving down the New York State Thruway, fifty state police cars deep, with lights and sirens blaring. We were bumper to bumper, lighting up the night sky as we rushed to Ground Zero. From behind the convoy, it looked like a fire-breathing dragon weaving through a countryside.

Once we hit the George Washington Bridge leading into the city, the view of the skyline reminded us all of why we'd driven from every corner of the state. Smoke from smoldering debris and the smell of burning jet fuel permeated the air as we made our way closer to the crash site. An eerie quietness crawled through the alleys of the dark gray skyscrapers and high-rise apartment buildings lining the streets. A city, which was normally bursting at the seams with pedestrians and yellow taxicabs, had become a ghost town. It felt like NYC had died - that is, until we reached the West Side Highway nearing the heart of Manhattan. Hundreds of New Yorkers stood in the center median that divided the north and southbound traffic, waving and holding American flags. The crowd cheer us on and thanked us for coming to help.

In that moment, there were no blacks, Hispanics, Jews, women, men, Whites, atheists, or Christians. That day, we were just human beings, joined together by the devastation that filled every fiber of our hearts. All veils dissolved; all pretenses, surface colors, and backgrounds unifying for the sake of humanity. Through all of the anger, pain, and sadness, my chest swelled with deep pride for being an American. For the first time in my life, I felt true unity. Whatever differences we had that pitted American against American were set aside, that day. We all needed each other, and I was honored to help in the cause. When people ask me if I think things will ever change concerning racism and discrimination in our country, I can say that it did once, and I was a part of it.

*To my brothers and sisters of the New York City Fire Department (FDNY), New York City Police Department (NYPD), New York State Police, and Emergency Response Teams from every agency, volunteers who fed us and the families who lost loved ones on that fateful day: For one moment in time, the earth stood still as we stood shoulder to shoulder and showed the world what humanity and love for thy neighbor truly means. Our stand together illustrated the essence of diversity.*

I saw diversity in action again when the floods of Hurricane Katrina wiped out entire sections of New Orleans. Although media reports focused on the looting and violence that occurred, my experience was completely different. Having been personally assigned as one of a select group of New York State Troopers, I patrolled the streets with officers from New Orleans who had lost everything to the floods. I worked with people from all walks of life who came together in support of each other. After my assignment during 9/11, I thought I'd never experience carnage and destruction of such magnitude again, but as I patrolled the streets of the 3$^{rd}$ and 9$^{th}$ wards in New Orleans, that thought was erased. The force of floodwaters washed entire neighborhoods away, leaving only concrete slab foundations. Black mold covered the insides of houses like crushed velvet and the smell of decay was thick enough to taste with every constricted breath I took.

These people had almost nothing left materially, but were willing to share what little they had with us. I never ate so much gumbo, crawfish, and boudin (a sausage made of several different types of meats and secret ingredients), in all my life! Every officer came to work each night with these strange, indescribably great tasting meals that smelled up the stations like a summer cookout. Without hesitation they invited each of us to share their meals and experience Southern hospitality. If I hadn't heard about the history of slavery and racism in the south, I wouldn't have believed it existed there. Our demographics (race, sex, religion, etc.) didn't impede our ability to work together. The crisis allowed each of us to use our unique talents to solve the many issues we faced in trying to restore a city, which had been decimated. As a former member of the NYSP, it was an honor to have been requested by the City of New Orleans to assist their law enforcement agency in re-establishing order. It's one of the greatest highlights of my career as a public servant. Experiences like these have kept me from making sweeping judgments about people and their abilities. When diversity is allowed to work its magic, small things become larger rewards as our horizons expand. Allowing ourselves to take risks by stepping out of the box society has put us all in gives us opportunities to explore and make connections with people we would otherwise avoid.

    I don't want to mislead anyone into thinking that I've learned all there is to know on the subject because there isn't a finite level of knowledge in this area. There's no fifth degree black-belt status or thirty-three degrees of knowledge on this topic. But I've studied it long enough to discover that it's much more than the recognition of physical traits and a few clichés like "diversity of thought." We all think differently, no matter what color, race, or sex we happen to be so that's not hitting the mark. Besides - if you're not wanted in the workplace anyway, who cares about your thoughts? What's more important to consider when it comes to diversity is: whose thoughts are included when it's time to make decisions on issues? Should decisions made by one group determine the actions for all? Do we as people decide that we'd rather fail at our goals and missions with our own kind rather than win with the ideas and principals of those who are different from us? These are the types of questions that must be addressed in order to incorporate diversity into the workplace.

My purpose is not to prove that diversity is perfect or a "must have" for success; but rather, to express how I've come to understand it as a necessary concept that can help identify, cultivate, and retain talent without sacrificing high standards. This isn't an editorial on racism or discrimination, either. Although they've both played critical roles in shaping my experiences, they are topics of great complexity and should be explored independently of one another.

I felt it imperative to show the application of diversity through first-hand experience as an employee, supervisor, and diversity practitioner because it allows me to illustrate the one thing that often goes unanswered, which is how to apply the concept in the workplace. To rely solely on theory or someone else's experience is like an athlete being coached by someone who's never played the game. Diversity is an individual journey with its own pace and consciousness. It can't be forced. Each person has to start from wherever they are. As a practitioner, I must meet people where they are and give them the time and space to process my message in a manner which applies to them. I can't make readers feel my experiences as a black man in America, neither can I force anyone to accept my opinions. I leave that to you as readers to decide whether the concepts and ideas I'm expressing make sense. My duty is to gain insight into what drives belief systems because I'm not only focused on helping people understand the concept, but I also want to show them how it works.

I'm convinced that most of society misunderstands the concept of diversity. I see signs of it everywhere due to the heavily-used demographic preferential hiring practices many companies and organizations rely on to create what they think are diversity initiatives. This is especially true in the area of diversity and equal employment opportunity (EEO) positions. Do a search of any company or business and if you see a heterosexual White male in one of these positions, cut the picture out and save it because it's rare to find. White men don't need my defense, and I'm not offering it. My point here is that because of discrimination and other phobias that White men have been immune to in the workplace, special consideration is given to women, minorities, and the LGBT community when it comes to hiring people for these positions. It's as though we've convinced ourselves that since minorities, women, and people of the LGBT community are the only ones being discriminated against, "let's let them have those jobs." That's great! For Affirmative Action, that is. To this day, I find myself repeatedly explaining the difference between diversity and Affirmative Action. To be clear, Affirmative Action does play a role in diversity, but the problem is that people use these terms synonymously when they are really completely different processes.

This book is designed to clarify the concept of diversity as a workplace necessity and give the reader a deeper appreciation of how it should be used. I will share with you how I came to understand the concept, using my twenty-seven years of military experience, twenty-plus years as a New York State Trooper, and seventeen years as both an

Equal Employment Specialist and a diversity consultant. By the end, I hope you will have learned what diversity is and how to utilize it for your own success. This is my story.

*I was fortunate to have two careers where performance could never be seen as a luxury. As a law enforcement officer and member of the military, high performance is a bona fide job requirement because lives are at stake at every moment. When you need people to come through and when you depend on the person next to you to get you home safely from a deployment or tour of duty, you stop thinking about what they look like and focus on what they can do. The nature of my jobs gave me a vested interest in learning the importance of incorporating different skill sets, life experiences, and abilities into the workplace. Within every facet of American society, diversity plays a role, and we are all players in its success or failure. As you read this book, I will illustrates how it all ties together and show how to implement it into any organization.*

# PART 1

# 1

## DESTINATION DIVERSITY

### Born This Way

I grew up in the '60s, not long after the Civil Rights Bill of 1964 was signed and Dr. Martin Luther King Jr. was assassinated for his efforts in pursuing equality for black people in America. Images of race riots and civil rights marches depicted harsh realities for blacks in this country. This was just a preview of what society would have in store for me. The reality of how I'd be treated as a black man couldn't be captured in a photo or short television segment. No one told me that these were just vignettes of a never-ending horror movie and that I'd play a starring role. My birth into the world gave me a mandatory ticket to watch the exorcism of blacks and other minorities who didn't fit into the neat little boxes society had assembled. Life was limited for us, and we had to learn how to survive under restraints and restrictions. We had no nice manicured lawns with white picket fences nor the freedom to run the streets and play without being warned by parents to watch what we said and how we carried ourselves in public. We were told to assimilate at all cost: Don't make White people uncomfortable, or else you would cause your own demise. Most of us followed these rules and made out okay. As a young child, it's easy to miss all the drama around you while watching cartoons and playing kickball.

Once I graduated from high school and left the safe surroundings of my small, yet diverse, city on the shores of Lake Erie, I was no longer seen as the nice kid on the block who went to church, starred in athletics, got good grades, and liked by teachers liked. In the eyes of America, as the rap icon and movie producer Ice Cube put it: "My skin was my sin." Merely being born a black man made me "The Super Predator" Hillary Clinton spoke of when her husband Bill Clinton passed the controversial crime bill in 1994. The "Violent Crime Control and Law Enforcement Act" was the largest crime prevention act in the history of the United States. It included provisions such as the "Three Strikes Rule" which carried a life sentence for repeat offenders, funds to hire one hundred thousand new law enforcement officers, 9.7 billion dollars in funding for prisons, and an expansion of death penalty-eligible offences.[i] What made the bill controversial were claims that it was responsible for decimating black communities. The number of black men sent to prisons for non-violent crimes such as the possession or sale of marijuana and small amounts of illegal narcotics grew rapidly. Those convicted were mostly young black and

Hispanic men between the ages of eighteen and thirty-five; prime ages for solidifying professional success and creating family stability.

There was no doubt that crime in the early '90s was at all-time highs in urban areas. The crack-cocaine epidemic plagued many black communities and created cause for action. It was a double-edge sword that cut straight through the fabric of urban neighborhoods. Black men were seen as drug-dealing savages who weren't considered human. Due to my skin color, I was seen that way, too. Although I'd never been to jail, the chains of isolation and rejection around my neck were squeezing the life out of me. I was just another black male no one recognized for any special reason, other than the stereotypes people had about us: criminal-minded, lazy, sexually aggressive ... the list goes on. Growing up and going out on my own was like being born all over again. The fluids of life that protected me in my mother's womb had been wiped from my eyes and I could see life in HD. The world was a scary place I'd only heard about from my parents, but up until now hadn't experienced. I couldn't imagine so many people would be afraid of me. If I walked through a parking lot, every White woman who caught a glimpse of my dark skin locked her car doors in fear. It sounded like a symphony, with every lock hitting its note at the precise time. Like a conductor draped in a black tuxedo, I didn't have to say a word. My presence said it all. Sometimes I played to their fears and sped up my pace to hear the rhythm of the locks change - "click click; click click clack." It was the only thing I could do to suppress the anger and resentment I felt. Was I a monster or something? I sure felt like it.

Often I'd try putting on a different face - one that wasn't scary to White people - but this never seemed to work. A smile could get you accused of sexual innuendos, a frown was considered menacing, and a blank stare meant you were crazy and about to assault someone. Try as I might, there was nothing I could do to change my circumstances; but I did put forth the effort. The mirror and I became familiar with each other. We'd have conversations about different approaches I should take. I would ask the mirror: "So how can I not look so threatening?" "Well you have to change your complexion." "Huh, my complexion! How can I do that?" "Well, you can use chemicals to lighten your skin" "Won't that burn?" "Of course it will; but hey, you'll be more acceptable, even to other blacks! Remember: light skin is special, and all the girls like it, too." "That's not going to work. I don't want to get burned. Give me something else." "Okay, try making those juicy lips of yours a little smaller and do something to narrow that nose. You look too - how can I put it - "black." Much too threatening." "Are you kidding me? Who'd do something like that?" "Young man, you'd be surprised. Just wait till you become a professional; you'll see what I mean." "Okay, well that ain't happening; my momma loves my wide nose and juicy lips. She tells me I'm handsome - so, no way! Next." "Okay, okay; this one I promise you can do without much effort. Switch to wearing collared polo shirts with little animals sewn on the chest. Get yourself some khakis and a pair of boat shoes - brown, so as to not be too flamboyant. Socks are optional, but if you really want to fit in, roll your pant legs at the bottom and tie a sweater around your neck!" "Alright! Finally: something I can do without changing my features!"

Later that week, I had a bone to pick with my reflective friend: "Man.... why did you tell me to dress like that?" "It's the American way, son; what do you mean? It shows that you're a safe one. Civilized, so to speak." "Civil! I almost got my butt kicked at school today. Not to mention I almost passed out during chemistry class. Those rolls you told me to put at the bottom of my pants cut off my circulation and my legs went numb. Then my hands fell asleep from those tight sleeves on the li'l shirt with collar you suggested. I'm not built for this, man!" "Well, kiddo, you never asked if these changes were right for you. You only asked how not to look so threatening. Don't be mad at me. I'm just a mirror."

If it weren't for me having two loving parents who insisted I be nothing less than the best person I could be, chances are I would've been a broken young man. I could've easily given up and just accepted that the country I lived in wasn't created for black people. I could've blamed the world and every White person in it for all of my failures and disappointments. This wasn't, and isn't, the case. Even though I experienced these things, I also experienced growing up attending school with some cool White kids who had some cool parents. They never displayed racist views in my presence or treated me as if I were different. I never heard them use the word nigger, and none of them ignored me or my family in public the way people often do when they're not comfortable with you. I learned early on that no matter what is happening around me to judge people by what they do, not by who they are. Actions determine character.

I refused to be broken by the racism and hatred that crushed the wills and destroyed the dreams of so many people of color. I was going to do better than what society expected of me. Since I believed in God, I couldn't wrap my head around the idea of another human being able to control my destiny. I developed a motto: "If you didn't make me, you couldn't break me." I don't recall where it came from or how I began to recite it, but that's what I'd say to myself when confronted with racism and bigotry. I vowed that no one would ever make me ashamed to be who I was. I had to choose whether to assimilate and try to fit in with the dominant group, or stay true to myself using the lessons my parents engrained in me and my siblings, like keeping our heads high and being proud of our heritage. I chose the latter, and it was the best decision I ever made. Staying true to myself gave me the freedom to explore the world at my own pace, without the boundaries of fitting into the status quo. Society gave me the solitude I needed to analyze every aspect of human relations by keeping me on the outside of the mainstream of what was acceptable in America. I was alone with no mentors or blueprints handed down to help me navigate my way through the world. This was a journey I had to travel alone and in so doing, I found my passion in life: teaching diversity.

**Timing is everything**

I joined the Air Force in 1988 at the height of the equal opportunity movement. The Federal Government had begun enforcing some of its Affirmative Action policies and organizations were beginning to feel the pressure from lawsuits leveled at them for discriminatory hiring practices. The work environment was changing, and I was right in the middle of it. In 1992, I completed my tour of duty and became a New York State Trooper. I was in my twenties, enjoying life and trying to figure out my place in the world. At the same time, a push for equality was being mounted to bring women and minorities into the workplace. According to

Malcolm Gladwell, author of such books as Outliers, Blink, and David and Goliath, my timing couldn't have been better.

In the book "Outliers," Mr. Gladwell asserts that the timing of a person's birth is key to their success in a particular field. Bill Gates, for example, was born in the '50s, making him a teenager when the first computer was introduced to the public. He was able to spend thousands of hours on the world's first computers because his mother worked for the school system, which had a connection to the university where the computers were located. This allowed Gates to get a head start in the world of computer technology, and before society knew what was happening, he and a few pioneers of the industry revolutionized computers and changed the course of the world. I'm not claiming to be the next Bill Gates. I'm Gary Richardson born in 1967 during the infancy of Civil Rights, Affirmative Action, and equal opportunity in America. Perfect timing for me to learn the process that would later be identified as diversity.

This new concept was introduced off the heels of Affirmative Action, which focused on ridding the country of the pervasive racism blacks experienced in the '60s and '70s. White males in particular saw Affirmative Action as a form of professional castration, cutting off their control over the work environment. It made for turbulent but exciting times for me. My military and law enforcement careers became laboratories for studying human relations. In hyper-aggressive careers like these, White men had no problem expressing anger and resentment towards outsiders. Women need not apply unless they were willing to subject themselves to the vulgarity of a prison yard and sexist jokes that would offend even the criminals we arrested. After hearing the criticism and derogatory comments long enough, I asked myself, "Why would women and minorities choose to stay in organizations, which despised them so much?" I began to wonder if I'd been hired based on my skills, or just to satisfy some social experiment. After all, I only had to pass an entrance exam, a physical fitness test, and, in the case of the State Police, manage to make it through a background investigation.

I'm not minimizing the process because it was tough and required immeasurable patience. Some recruits were on the 'eligible hire list' for up to four years, hoping to be selected. Many of them couldn't wait that long for a job and found employment elsewhere. Passing the written exam and making it through the background investigation still didn't guarantee that I or anyone else would be successful in either organization, but it was part of the process we all had to complete. I couldn't grasp the motivation behind why I'd been hired, other than for my physical characteristics. Many Whites seemed to be asking the same question. Once I began my careers, I found that some of my co-workers equated my worth as just another Affirmative Action hire. This was made clear when some of them suggested it was easier for minorities and women to become troopers since the "standards" had been lowered. This is a common statement made whenever organizations decide to hire women and minorities. People who weren't Troopers would say things like: "I have a friend who's retiring from the State Police because they're hiring people who can't even read!" When I say 'heard', I mean firsthand. It was said to me after my naiveté got the best of me and I excitedly revealed that I'd been accepted into the State Police Academy. Somehow I missed the memorandum that I'd become illiterate overnight. It's a good thing I could read well enough to understand the acceptance letter.

While at the academy, I felt like I held the fate of the entire black population on my shoulders. If I failed, it would be a group failure, confirming the negative stereotypes of people who were said to be incapable of performing complex tasks. Every time I performed I lost ten pounds from sweating so much. It was due to the anxiety of failing. I knew I had the ability to be a good law enforcement officer, but the stereotypes and low expectations of blacks had both positive and negative psychological effects on me. The stress of not being right, making mistakes, or failing a test, made me study all there was to know about being an officer. Unfortunately, I couldn't unlearn my blackness. The same chocolate brown skin that made my parents so proud had turned into a plague. It made people stop talking whenever I walked into a room; made them stop whatever it was they were doing and stare. No "hello", no "can I help you" - just blank, wide-eyed stares. I was beginning to understand why my parents worried about me and my brother's futures as young black men. My parents were born in the South twenty years before the civil rights movement, and experienced legalized institutional racism in every aspect of their lives. From segregated school systems to public water fountains specifically labeled for blacks, they went through it all.

From the time I was a child, I was well aware that my skin color would fill my life with challenges. It was as common then as it is today for black parents to warn their children about the negative perceptions people had concerning skin color. Just ask a middle-aged black person what the "paper-bag" test was used for. Don't worry; this is nothing like saying the word "nigger." It won't cause a riot. Those old enough to know will tell you that it was a means by which to measure acceptance. Growing up, there was a belief that if a black person was lighter than a brown paper bag, they were considered tolerable to society. To be clear: tolerated, but not fully accepted. Our elders told us this idea was adopted during the course of slavery as a result of White slave owners impregnating black slaves. This produced light-skinned children who were looked at as being better than darker-skinned blacks. They were treated better, too. They were often referred to as the 'House Niggers' because they were used as servants who were allowed to work inside their master's homes.

*Who would have thought that a paper bag, light as a feather, carried so much weight?*

What I thought were silly little myths became reality. My complexion didn't pass the paper-bag test, so I thought it played a role in how I was perceived. It sounds crazy now to think that a person's value as a human was being determined by an item used to hold groceries, but in a society where color and race mean more than performance, it makes sense. This is where the first brick in the foundation of diversity was laid for me. I never bought into the belief that skin color, religion, or anything else predetermined a person's skills or abilities. As far as I was concerned, these were just man made categories created to keep people in their place. It was a power structure set up to pick and choose who and what was acceptable. I knew I had talent that could be used to accomplish great things. I knew others did, too. I didn't want a career in law enforcement or the military because I was black; I wanted them because I knew I could do the job well. It became my personal quest to show America what it was missing by not including the unique skill sets of all people. I would get my chance, but it would come in a way that I never imagined.

*Solitude can be a valuable tool for learning if you learn how to deal with the loneliness that comes with it. Being alone and questioning every decision and every move I made gave me time to analyze, design, develop, implement and evaluate a plan for getting ahead in the workplace. If this sounds familiar, it's the ADDIE model for instructional design. I didn't know it at the time, but I was forced to use it because I was alone; an outsider. This model would later play a key role in how I created the brand of diversity I teach to this day. I once read that a young black officer by the name of Henry O. Flipper, who was the first black to graduate from West Point Service Academy in 1877, went through his entire four years of college in complete solitude. No one spoke to him outside of the harsh treatment he received from his White classmates. Certainly, I could survive a little ostracism.*

# 2
# LAYING THE FOUNDATION

## A Diversity Practitioner is Born

The year was 1998 and I was about to take part in my first human relations class. It was a crisp fall day and the leaves on the trees were showcased like proud peacocks spreading their iridescent fan of feathers. If you've ever visited Upstate New York in the fall, you may've been fortunate enough to witness this spectacle. Vivid oranges, reds, yellows, fuchsias and purples lined the streets and highways like floats in a Macy's Day Parade. I just transferred from the 105th Airlift Wing in Newburgh, New York, about an hour north of NYC, and was now at Hancock Field Air Base in Syracuse, New York. I was excited to settle into this new environment and see what it had to offer. During those days, the bulk of workplace training focused on the unfair treatment of minorities; specifically, blacks. It was an attempt to bring cultural awareness into the workplace, but it was based mostly on negative stereotypes and discrimination. As part of the Air National Guard's mandatory training, each member had to receive at least four hours of human relations training, which included topics such as cultural awareness and equal opportunity.

While sitting in the class with about twenty other eager participants, I scanned the room and couldn't help but notice that aside from the black leather chairs surrounding the long oak table we were seated around, I was the darkest thing in the room. No big deal: I was used to being one of the few minorities, being a State Trooper. Besides, we were only going to be talking about how people should treat each other, and I was well versed on that from reading the Ten Commandments every Sunday at church. "Ye shall not bare false witness against thy neighbor" (meaning: don't lie about anyone), and "ye shall not kill." Too easy! All we needed to do was read these a few times and the class would be over. Growing up, it was mandatory in my household to attend not just church, but Sunday school, too. Every Sunday! I used to wish I had the power to create an Eleventh Commandment that said: "Thou shall not have to go to church every Sunday, especially if thou must waketh up at seven a.m. and walketh ten miles to get there!" My father believed that walking built character and strength, so by the time I was twelve, my legs were so strong I could've easily carried a freezer on my back. I laughed to myself, thinking how absurd it was for adults to have to sit through a formal class on how to treat people with dignity and respect. Now, after years of working in the fields of diversity and equal opportunity, I laugh at myself for thinking a course in human relations was absurd.

Suddenly the door flew open and in walked this 6' 7" White guy. His name was Major Mark Brady, the Director of what was known back then as the Social Actions Office. This was the office designated to facilitate Affirmative Action for minorities and women, but was more often used to conduct urinalysis screening to detect unlawful drug use. I kept waiting to see a black or Hispanic instructor walk through the door after him, but it never happened. I thought to myself: "What the hell is going on here?" How could this have anything to do with Affirmative Action or cultural awareness with this White dude teaching the course? I couldn't wait to hear what he had to say. To my surprise, he was very open about why 'his group' (White males) didn't view women and minorities in the workplace as being important. He explained that, for the most part, there wasn't anything significant enough in their encounters with minorities and women to change the negative perceptions concerning their abilities. In the diversity lexicon, this is referred to as a S.E.E., or 'significant emotional event;' something that occurs in a person's life that changes the way he or she feels about an issue. I paused for a moment and thought: "What a lame excuse. They're just racist!" By this time, I'd completely lost interest in the class. I was too mad to process anything. Everything that came out of his mouth sounded like Charlie Brown's teacher: "whomp, whomp, whomp, wa." I couldn't wait to ask him the $100,000 question: "How come you don't have any black people on your staff?"

Once he finished the presentation, I finally got what I was hoping for. "Does anyone have any questions?" My hand shot up like a kindergartener trying to be the first to be called on by the teacher. He acknowledged me and said, "Yes, Sergeant Richardson?" I replied with conviction: "Well, if this class is about human relations and culture, why don't you have any black people on your staff?" Dead silence fell over the room like a dark cloud. Some people dropped their heads in embarrassment while others turned fire engine red. I thought to myself, "Aha! I bet you weren't ready for that one, Mr. Larry Bird." Subconsciously, I had given him that name because he was a 6' 7" White guy just like the legendary Boston Celtic Larry Bird and looked more like he should've been playing professional basketball instead of teaching a class on human relations. His reaction was not what I expected. He looked at me with a smile and said: "Stick around after class. I'd like to talk to you about that." What? Talk about that? No stutter, no hesitation, no redness of the cheeks - nothing but a smile! A vision of an old cartoon popped in my mind, "The Road Runner." I saw myself as Wile E. Coyote as he chased the speedy bird through the desert, and just as he was about to catch him, the road suddenly went off the end of a cliff and Mr. Coyote found himself flailing in midair. That's exactly where I was: stuck in midair with the same terrified look on my face that Wiley had just before he crashed to the ground.

Analytical as I am, I thought long about what he meant by "talk with you about that." Somehow I knew *'that'* had something to do with *'me.'* My unconscious bias of thinking only minorities should teach all things about human relations led to a conversation between two men from very different walks of life, who ended up seeing eye-to-eye (or, rather, eye to chest, since I stand 5' 6" and him 6' 7"). Major Brady didn't waste time with small talk. He got right to the point and asked: "What unit are you in?" Anyone who's ever been in the military understands that when an enlisted member is told by a superior officer to wait after class, it typically spells disaster for the poor soul. Either you're in trouble or were about to receive a task that made you believe you were. Instead, I was given a blessing. I was introduced to the world of equal opportunity, which would be the catalyst for my career in diversity. I told the Major I was in the Civil Engineering Squadron and he replied, "You're in the wrong unit; you need to be over here." Major Brady called my bluff that day, and then asked me to join his staff.

## **The Talk**

At the time, there weren't many White guys working in the equal opportunity realm, and I wondered what made Major Brady go that route. Everyone in the military knew that a career in equal opportunity was a career killer. It wasn't a well-respected program and also not a position of command in which you're responsible for overseeing large numbers of military personnel. I asked him why he decided to go into this field, knowing how others viewed it. He simply said: "Gary, my group just doesn't get it! They don't understand equal opportunity, so as a White male, I have to be the one who tells them what it means." Brady felt that Whites in general, especially males, had a difficult time listening to blacks speak to them about equality. His reasoning was that he didn't believe most Whites ever saw blacks as being equal to them. I could see his point. There were once laws that didn't allow blacks to drink water from the same fountain as Whites, or sit in the front row of public establishments. My parents had already told me about their experiences living in the South with these laws, so what he was telling me sounded logical. I knew it was true, but I still thought it was idiotic. I said, "Sir, that's so stupid. If I tell the truth about discrimination and how it affects minorities, it should be more credible coming from me." In my mind, I figured that I was a respectable black man since I was a State Trooper and serving in the military. He chuckled and said: "Coming from someone black, the message of inequality is not received very well; it makes people relive the past." *The past! This happens every day*, I thought! I wondered how in the world people would ever get it. Better yet - how the heck would I be able to bridge this gap and help keep women and minorities from leaving the workplace out of frustration? What Mr. Brady told me was that I had a hurdle to jump. Right or wrong, I'd have to work harder to establish credibility, due to my color. He let me know that just because I had experience in this area didn't mean that Whites would accept what I had to say. I'd just have to do more: that's it. Life works that way sometimes. You can either complain about it and quit, or overcome the obstacles.

My stomach churned like an unbalanced washing machine with too many wet towels inside. How could it be so clear-cut that my race or color determined my abilities? It wasn't like this when I was a kid. I grew up in a diverse city with friends of every race, creed, and color. They liked and respected me for whom I was and what I had to say. I was captain of the football team, was popular around the community, and my teachers spoke highly of me. There was no way I was going to sit back and accept what he was telling me. Doing so would keep me locked in mental slavery; the kind of thinking that killed so many spirits. The stress of never being respected as a man and not being able to provide for our families - that kills us. Bullets, drugs, and alcohol are the residual effects of the real issues. I wouldn't settle for the status quo no matter how tough things got for me. If I was going to be on this earth for whatever time I was given, I had to get everything I could out of life. I had nothing to lose and everything to gain.

The anger from what Mr. Brady was telling me started to get the best of me. I could see how easy it was for a man to explode at someone for being disrespected and treated like he's worthless. To hear someone tell me that my feelings don't matter is a slap in the face. I held my anger and asked: "Okay, Sir, if what you're telling me is true, why did you pick me to join your staff?" He answered, "Because I see something in you, which resonates with people. I believe you can make a difference." He was referring to me teaching human relations classes like the one he'd just taught. Still, his reply didn't satisfy my angst. I felt like he was talking in riddles; like we were doing a remake of the TV show "Kung Fu" and I was playing David Carradine's role as Grasshopper. At the time, I couldn't make the connection between my ability to do things differently and how it would change people's perceptions about human relations. I knew there were people who'd never believe in equality no matter what message I presented, but I also knew that not every White person thought the same or ascribed to the same belief system. If that were the case, Mr. Brady wouldn't have existed and I would've been talking to a hologram. There were more people on earth besides blacks and Whites, and the military provided me with a demographic smorgasbord to learn from.

Major Brady wasn't putting everyone in the same box when he told me his group (White males) wouldn't listen to me because I was black. He was giving me a heads up for where the pushback against diversity would come from. He was priming me for the future. Unfortunately, he was only half right. In the years to come, I would learn that pushback would also come from some women and minorities. If that surprises you, join the team. When I first experienced it, I was caught off guard, too. During some of the training courses I've been in, women and minorities are sometimes the first to speak out against things like Affirmative Action and equal opportunity. Some of them feel uncomfortable talking about these topics for fear of being rejected by their White male counterparts.

Everything about Mr. Brady and his work represented diversity, but I didn't see it at the time. The lessons I took from our relationship were organic. I learned that we could look different, come from different places, have different upbringings, and even think differently; but still want equality for everyone. Our conversations were without structure, formality, or rigid expectations. I got to know him as Mark Brady and he knew me as Gary Richardson. He didn't have to pretend to understand the plight of blacks in America and I didn't have to pretend to be anything but myself, a black man. Over the years, Mark and I developed a professional relationship that, in its makeup, defines what I would later learn to be true diversity. Not only did he call my bluff by asking me to be on his staff, but he also confirmed something else. He did play basketball for years although not professionally or for the Celtics, like Larry Bird.

## **Limited Expectations**

When Mr. Brady walked into the classroom that day, he had no chance of reaching me with his message. I'd already mentally set the stage for the course. In my mind, a level of expectation developed that wouldn't allow me to see his true value on the topic he was teaching. I figured since the subject was on human relations and equal opportunity, it required a certain life experience, like being discriminated against not just on occasion, but on a daily basis. More to the point, I believed that a person of color, specifically a black person, should've been teaching the course. After all, Title

VII of the 1964 Civil Rights Act was written to protect the rights of minorities in this country and stop the pervasive discrimination blacks were experiencing. Leaders like Dr. Martin Luther King and Malcolm X led the movement, so I felt it was a black thing. The images I saw as a child emphasized the harsh treatment blacks experienced at the hands of Whites in America. The fact that Whites were beaten and murdered fighting for Civil Rights was rarely, if ever, shown. The first time I'd ever seen Whites being attacked was when I watched the movie "Mississippi Burning," a story about three young civil rights workers (two of whom were White) were kidnapped and killed by Ku Klux Klan members. I wondered why no one ever mentioned anything about Whites being killed. Not that I wanted White people to share in being murdered, but it was critical information left out of the conversation about the equal rights movement.

Not seeing Whites fighting for the cause allowed me to skip the science of diversity, which Mr. Brady was displaying. I thought it was about race and color instead of talents and abilities. He was using his unique experiences to educate our organization on human relations. I consciously made the decision that he shouldn't be teaching the class based on his demographics, and not his abilities. Since I only saw people who looked like me being attacked, it was natural for me to think it was our fight against hate and inequality, and no one else's. My thinking was that Black people had the legitimate right to own and operate anything dealing with equal rights. I didn't care about Mr. Brady's experience or what he could add to the conversation about equality. I saw him as the oppressor - the guy who had all the privilege in the world because of his color and sexual orientation. If the complete story of civil rights had been depicted to show everyone who marched and fought for it, I believe I would've been more accepting of him in his role. Instead, I took a FUBU mentality, thinking that if it was For Us, then it should be By Us.

## Win at all Cost

This mental conditioning I just described formed my initial expectation of Mr. Brady. If I had a place in society, then I felt that he had one, too. My personal biases kept me from being open to differences even when they could benefit me. It was the same 'stand your ground' mindset that seems to have plagued our political system: "Support the views of your party at all cost, no matter how ridiculous or divisive the ideas may be. Winning is all that matters." Mr. Brady was speaking from his experience as a White male; something I had no insight into, yet so easily dismissed. He was showing me pieces to the diversity puzzle, but I was missing it. I disregarded his value on the topic because he wasn't black or Hispanic. If this sounds like discrimination, you're right: it was.

## My Inheritance

No one had to send me a memorandum or certificate of ownership. I felt minorities were entitled to monopolize any subject that dealt with equality, culture, or human relations - just a little retribution for all of the hell we've been through since slavery. The government never gave us our forty acres and a mule as promised, but at least we could have some topics that belonged to us. Speaking of entitlements may sound ridiculous, but when people feel disenfranchised, what happens often. Think back to the O.J. Simpson trial, which occurred right after the Rodney King beating by the LAPD. The brutality of the arrest was caught on video and went viral before the term became fashionable. The officers in that case were found not guilty, and L.A. erupted into riots costing lives and millions of dollars worth of damage. Simpson's acquittal of the double homicide had less to do with evidence and everything to do with the "You owe us one" mentality. It's the most extreme example; but right or wrong, it explains the mindset of people excluded from the mainstream, and was the reason I felt the way I did about Mr. Brady teaching the class.

This is illustrates some of the obstacles I had to navigate through on the road to understanding diversity. The biases I had, whether conscious or unconscious, affected how much I was willing to accept the opinions and differences of others especially when I felt they were taking something away from me. If someone called me a racist for having these feelings, I would've easily disputed it. I would've denied that I ever discriminated against anyone based on race, color, or anything else; but that's exactly what I was doing. I didn't feel I was doing it because, in my mind, my feelings were justified. It was easy to rationalize things when it impacted me, but not so much when it affected someone else. Before I clearly understood diversity, none of it mattered - there was no way Mark Brady was more qualified than any black or Hispanic person on the subject. I didn't care what university he went to: as far as I was concerned, if he didn't graduate from the School of Hard Knocks or Penitentiary State University, he wasn't qualified to teach these topics.

## **Talent vs. Characteristics**

It would take me a few years to realize my feelings towards Mr. Brady teaching human relations was wrong. My views were literally written in black and white, us against them. This mentality I had grown accustomed to begun to change in 1999. My enlightenment took place when I met a world-renowned diversity consultant by the name of Dr. Samuel Betances. The Air National Guard contracted Dr. Betances to create a diversity-training program in support of the Guard's push to increase its diversity. I was fortunate to have been selected to go to Denver, Colorado and be trained as a facilitator for the program. Little did I know that when I asked Mr. Brady why there were no blacks on his staff, it would land me in Denver? The trip would also connect me with a lady who became my most important professional alley, Judith Mathewson. She was the facilitator of the group I was assigned to and would help push my military career to heights I never imagined. I will discuss her significance in the section on mentorship later in this book. If you have to be sent anywhere, Denver isn't a bad place to be banished to. It's a beautiful city.

Dr. Botances taught me that looks didn't matter when it came to diversity! What did matter were the talents and skills people brought to table. He'd say: "It's not about counting heads, but making heads count!" In laymen's terms; stop counting how many women and minorities you've collected and instead, utilize their talents to help the organization. This was my epiphany. The flame of diversity comprehension was lit and It began to burn inside of me like an inferno. Until Dr. Betances, everything I'd heard talked about groups of people (minorities and women or "them") as though we were aliens and the world had to prepare for our arrival. It made everyone uncomfortable, including the minorities and women attending the classes. It felt like they were being identified as "Those poor people who've been treated so badly. Let's be fair and give them some of our privilege." It was embarrassing, and made people want to hide in a corner. Blacks and other minorities don't need pity. They need opportunities and jobs. As a black man, I was tired of listening to how racism and discrimination affected minorities without any realistic solutions to address the problem. If I was tired of it, I knew others were tired, too. Early practitioners of diversity training were trying to explain the concept as a method for curing social ills. The problem with this approach was that moralistic principles like treating people with dignity, being sensitive to their feelings, and respecting different cultures didn't illustrate how doing so would increase profits. There was no business or work-related reason given other than "do it or you will be sued" or "do it because it's the right thing to do." Organizations weren't being told to do these things to attract a diverse customer base or to enhance ideas by incorporating a mix of ideas and perspectives. Those attributes of diversity weren't introduced until years later. This is a reason diversity training got such a bad rep and still has one today. Employees had no reason to feel that all the hoopla about diversity training would help their businesses or organizations become successful. There was no link to performance. It was difficult to make the argument that companies and organizations wouldn't be successful without women and minorities, since they already had been. Feeling sorry for someone wasn't making companies money or boosting productivity. If it didn't make dollars, it didn't make sense. There wasn't much data on the subject considering the concept was so new. No one could point to any meaningful research to support it, making it impossible to show that it was of any benefit. I admit that I was stumped, too. How did equal opportunity relate to productivity, and what role did diversity play in all of this? If I couldn't find the answers, I'd be just another minority asking people to feel sorry for us.

*What Dr. Betances did was make me begin to see the meaning of inclusion and its importance to diversity. Without it, you're just counting heads. I thought back to when I was a child in elementary school when during recess we would all play kickball or some athletic activity. As cruel as it was, no one wanted the kid who was awkward and couldn't play well. We had no reason to want him or her on the team other than the teacher saying that everyone had to play. He or she would be the last to get a turn, laughed at for not performing well, and beaten up for making the team lose. They simply didn't count! No one took the time to cultivate any potential talent they might have had, and they were too afraid to show any if they had it. The workplace is the same, for people who aren't accepted in society. Since we don't leave our values and beliefs in the parking lot, they accompany us into the workplace and impede our judgments on the ways we interact with people. We only want to count them, not include them.*

# 3

# EXPOSING THE BARRIERS

## By the Numbers

As my self-study on the concept of diversity grew, I noted a lot of emphasis was being placed on the number of women and minorities in the workplace (or the lack thereof). Although numbers told a story, they didn't include enough insight as to why, after all the efforts to hire more women and minorities, the numbers remained so low. Women and minorities were being hired like never before, and the landscape of the workplace was changing. The problem was, as fast as they arrived, they were leaving. There was no plan to engage them and keep them around. The money being thrown at cultural awareness training was going to waste, and consultants were gobbling it up. Although I was an average student in math, it didn't take me long to recognize that the numbers would never add up. According to census data, blacks only made up around thirteen percent of the total population. How could we be represented by that same percentage across all work sectors? How could every company, business, and organization attain and maintain a thirteen percent black workforce? Let's not forget women have always made up almost fifty-one percent of the entire United States population - should they make up fifty-one percent of the total workforce in order to have diversity? It's not possible. Job requirements alone would eliminate large groups of people due to the specialized skill sets required. Others would self-eliminate for lack of interest in certain career fields, making that thirteen or fifty-one percent even more difficult to achieve. What would be the magic number for successfully achieving diversity if it was based on counting heads, as Dr. Botances warned against? Number crunching was just one problem. The other was fear of change.

*Quantity vs. quality has always been a question surrounding diversity, but not in the right context for its success. Detractors who feel that minorities and women are less qualified than White men posed it. Although I could argue all day about the weaknesses of their position, the question itself is a legitimate one. Is it better to have more people, or to have more quality work from people? I found that the latter was easier when people were selected or hired because of their abilities. Because of the racism and discrimination occurring in many workplaces, I knew that it would be an uphill battle to change mindsets on this issue. It's difficult to convince people that 'others' whom they have no connection with (and may despise) have something of value to bring into the organization. I would have to figure this out, or organizations would continue to count heads and waste millions of dollars doing so.*

## **Fear of Change**

When I returned from Denver, I saw things from a different perspective. I began to study Dr. Bentances' program and became more intrigued by this thing called diversity. Unfortunately, it never got off the ground. For reasons unknown to me, the Air National Guard abandoned the training program, and I was left out in the cold with a bunch of VHS and cassettes tapes to add to my collection of Parliament and Funkadelic eight tracks. It couldn't have happened at a worse time. The workplace was evolving, and people weren't sure how to react to the dynamic shifts created by working in demographically diverse workplaces. All wasn't lost on the training I'd received, though. It helped me prepare ways to address some of the future challenges the military was about to experience. Dr. Betances' training took me to the point of not counting heads, but I would need to add more to my repertoire to deal with the anxiety created by the rapid changes occurring in the workplace. This anxiety was not exclusive to White men, either. Everyone was afraid of change, and I was about to experience just how much.

After some extraordinary events, which I will explain later, I was assigned to the Social Actions Office and became part of Major Brady's staff. By this time, the office had been renamed to the Military Equal Opportunity Office, and I was about to get my shot at doing things differently, as Major Brady had proposed. I was in the driver's seat now, and it was my responsibility to design and teach the Human Relations Training program. One day while teaching a class, the opportunity to deal with the anxiety I mentioned jumped up and smacked me in the face. A young black man stood up in the middle of the class and went on a rant, expressing his anger concerning the abolishment of the military's "Don't

Ask, Don't Tell" policy. This was the military's controversial stance on homosexuality within the armed forces. Prior to it being abolished, being openly gay in the military was strictly prohibited. If discovered, a member would be discharged immediately. This young brother, who looked to be in his early twenties, protested having to room or shower with a gay male, fearing the person might be attracted to him. In the back of my mind I couldn't help but think, "Really, dude? You ain't no Denzel Washington!" I was relieved that he couldn't read my mind. Since he looked so young, I assumed he hadn't experienced discrimination like someone from the baby boomer generation may have. I took the liberty of informing him that, once upon a time, the same anger and resentment he was expressing was aimed at people who looked like him - that once there were "*Jim Crow*" laws that legalized segregation and discrimination with things like "White only" sections in public places. I went further to explain that when anyone, no matter what race, color, or creed, tried to push back against these unjust laws, they were met with the same anger and resentment he was expressing towards gays. His eyes widened and jaw dropped as if to say, "How appalling - those damn White people." When fear becomes anger, it's almost impossible to empathize with another person's plight. My hunger to learn the concept of diversity made me slow down and ask myself; "What if I were in their shoes?"

*Empathy was one of the most important skills I acquired on my journey to understanding diversity. Empathy doesn't require agreement. It requires compassion and a hunger to learn the viewpoints of others. Unless I was able to see someone else's point of view, I would never be able to present my message in a way they could understand and relate to. It would come from one perspective: my own.*

*Empathy allowed me to approach issues concerning human relations from different angles. It enabled me to use examples and analogies that people were familiar with. I wanted to feel the fears, resentment and concerns of others, just as I had my own. I also wanted to feel their happiness! What made the detractors of equality feel happy about the lives they were living? Were their ambitions the same as mine? Did they like the work they were doing? It was critical for me to know these things before I could clarify diversity and alleviate some of the problems it created - problems created because the process of implementing it into the workplace was ineffective and broken. In most cases, it caused more anger and resentment. It negatively impacted work climates, making it difficult for people to work together harmoniously. It was time for me to assess the matter, and the best way to do it was by studying the ways of the dominant group: How they spoke to each other, how they managed conflict, what made them angry, and what they valued the most. Empathy was the only way to achieve it.*

## **Changing Places**

I began to wonder how I'd feel if the roles were reversed - if black people were the dominant race and I was forced to work with people I had no connection with - people whom society said were inferior to me and not quite human. I asked myself if I'd want to share my lifestyle with "those people." If my world taught me to believe they couldn't be trusted and weren't smart enough to be successful in life, would I want to engage with them? If roles were reversed and blacks were the dominant race, I might look at highly successful White people like Steve Jobs or Bill Gates and think: "If they made it, why can't other Whites?" It would've been easy for me to rationalize the conditions of those "poor white folks," since a few extraordinary individuals had made it ("If they just worked hard like Gates and Jobs, they'd be successful, too."). This is the rationalization that allows the dominant group to avoid the real reasons behind the lagging economic status, lower education levels, poverty, and discrimination that minorities experience on a daily basis. All of these are real issues, but they have real causes too, like institutional discrimination, racial profiling, and a refusal to hire minorities when they're qualified. But, I wouldn't have to consider those things because I wouldn't experience them being a member of the dominant group. Neither would I want to mix with people who did. I'd think they were just making excuses for being lazy. They would never be seen as equal to me.

If the world was created to benefit blacks and we were the gold standard for all of civilization, I would likely judge others according to my life experience. Seeing a few extremely successful White individuals would give me an out from ever facing the truth about how my group (blacks) rejoiced in so much privilege that we didn't know life was different for anyone else. I wouldn't feel guilty about it because I was born into it and all I knew. That's if things were different and roles were reversed. They're not, of course; but if they were, I'd probably feel that way.

I wondered if other groups of people felt exiled from the American Dream, too; cut off from being able to rise to the highest levels of their abilities. This is where things became a little strange. I discovered the answer was "yes," and in a way, I was responsible for it. I belonged to a group that had the ultimate privilege of ruling over everything on the planet. The group = men! We hold nearly all of the power, all of the wealth, and all of the influence in the world.

You name it we own it. What a sweet deal! I could even use the Bible, Koran, and every other book on religion to claim my power as being legit and unquestionable. God said so! I was literally the "man" - no kidding; this was fantastic! As a man, I didn't have to do a thing to earn the privileges that came along with the package. Take that however you wish. It didn't matter that I was black, either. If I played the game of life right, my gender gave me legitimate power over nearly every facet of life. I had privilege and loved it!

## **Gender Trumps Race**

In 2008, and again in 2016, America authenticated this privilege by choosing to elect a black man in President Barack Obama and an older one in President Donald Trump over Hillary Clinton. The fact that Barack Obama is multiracial had little bearing on the decision to elect him over a woman. The majority of people saw him as black. Gender trumped skin color in this case, and it probably wouldn't have mattered which woman ran against him. In 2016, it was confirmed again with the election of Donald Trump. Barring any conversation about possible collusion with Russia to win the election, let's be honest: a lot of women voted for Trump too. There were enough women who openly stated that they wouldn't vote for Hillary simply on the bases of her being a woman. I began to feel that America wasn't ready to be led by any woman. It was also confirmed while on my travels to different military bases. I'd hear men and women alike make statements against having a woman as Commander in Chief of the world's most powerful military. Some would say, "There's no way a woman can lead us in battle." From a male perspective, that sort of thinking eliminates half the competition. If it's accepted that women can't lead in situations such as war, then naturally, men are the only choice.

Not until a serious threat from a competent woman came about did I ever think about the privileges I have compared to them. Forget that Secretary Clinton had more experience for the role of President than nearly all the former Presidents before her. Forget that her husband had been President for two terms. Women didn't matter much in the circle of power and influence. That alone was my privilege as a man. Secretary Clinton's challenge for the Presidency was my wakeup call. Another player had entered the game (women), which spelled more competition. This was the same challenge White males were facing. The fear of losing power to minorities caused some otherwise - good people to protest in anger, blaming everything from too much government oversight to immigration as the cause of their woes. The privilege of being a man completely outweighed skills and abilities Hillary Clinton possessed.

Searching for the real meaning of diversity opened my eyes to the hidden privileges I enjoyed throughout my life. If I wanted to be acknowledged for my talents in spite of my race or color, I'd need to acknowledge that my female counterparts must have the same considerations when it came to gender. The discovery made me push the envelope of self-assessment. Once I did, I realized that although blacks had experienced hell on earth by the way we were (and still are) being treated, I had privileges as a man. At the same time as I felt the sting of racism, I also enjoyed the benefits of being male. In most cases, women are still paid less than men even when they are more educated and have more experience. When I looked at the privileges Whites had over me, I saw it as being unfair. I wasn't silly enough to believe I enjoyed the same privileges as White men, but I did have some. Until now, I never took the time to recognize the advantages I had over women in society but once I did, I had to be honest with myself and ask: "Had I fought just as hard for their equality as I had for my own?"

## **Unconscious Biases**

Unconscious biases are like alligators; more dangerous when hidden beneath the surface. My lack of understanding the privileges I had as a man made it easy for me to overlook the talents women brought to the workplace. The institutions I belonged to, gave me all the reasons I needed to discount them. The military had policies that legally denied women from joining combat units. No one ever told me why they weren't allowed, and they didn't need to. I accepted it because it wasn't my issue. I'd been socialized to view women as being physically and mentally weaker than men. That meant that I could and would always see them as weaker than me. Eventually, I assumed that the things women were kept from doing, were things they couldn't do. I didn't consider that quite possibly they could do those things, but weren't given the opportunity. It was a self-fulfilling prophecy, which repeated itself so often I didn't realize that, on many occasions, I was telling women to shut the hell up and sit down. Not literally; but whenever I took part in speaking over them in meetings, dismissing their ideas, or shrugging them off as if they didn't know what they were talking about, I was actually telling them to shut the hell up. I would never deliberately tell a woman that, but subconsciously my group (men) and I did it constantly by ignoring what they had to contribute to the organization. Worse we'd let them speak, not acknowledge what they were saying, then turn around and repeat it to receive standing ovations for the great idea we'd just come up with. When that happened to me, I would be furious and wouldn't hesitate to shout: "That's what I just said!" Even though I may have been the only black person in the room, I would take back my credit and talk about the jerk who tried to steal it. I never saw a women do that. If they did, they wouldn't be around long. "She's just too emotional," the guys would say.

Unconscious biases aren't always based on race or gender differences either. I would see women display biases against women and minorities be biased against people from their own race. There were women supervisors I knew who were much tougher on their female subordinates then they were on the men. The same was true for minorities. I've had black supervisors that went out of their way to chastise and belittle other blacks worse than any White person. When this happens, women and minorities who let their biases rule their judgment are more dangerous to their own kind than any White male could ever be. When a woman supervisor or leader speaks negatively about other women, or a minority does it to another in the workplace, that negativity is going to stick. People will say there's no way it could be discrimination or racism because they're from the same group! On the flip side, subordinates would often treat their same race or same gender supervisors and coworkers with less respect, for the same reasons. They had biases that made them feel they could get away with it because supervisors in these groups are less valued in many organizations.

It wasn't until I began to learn that diversity is more than demographic representation that I realized I had unconscious biases. When I started looking at ways to make heads count, the barriers to making diversity applicable to the workplace began to reveal themselves. Every dismissive gesture and every choice I made (like going through a checkout line in a store which had a black cashier) was a bias. My subconscious sent messages to my conscious mind that somehow familiarity was better - even safer. I didn't consider that maybe the person I avoided had more in common with me, or had unique talents that could benefit me. Like the time I needed to get a haircut while on military duty. I took pride in cutting my own hair and always carried my own clippers with me. Unfortunately, the one time I needed a cut in a rush, I'd forgotten them at home. Over to the base barber I went; and, just my luck, the only seat open was staffed by this young White dude with tattoos on top of tattoos. His face was even tatted up. First thought: Oh, no! This skinhead isn't cutting *my* hair. He must have felt my nervousness because he cleaned his chair for an extra ten minutes while I paced back and forth, calling myself all kinds of names for forgetting my clippers and ending up in this predicament. Oh well, the difference between a good haircut and a bad one is two weeks of hair growth. That's the crazy stuff my brothers would say after we got our soup-bowl haircuts we hated so much. I finally sat down, and every time the dude turned the clippers on, we both thought of some silly stuff to talk about, trying to delay the process. We finally ran out of things to say about the weather, and the adventure began. I kept my eyes closed, pretending I was sleep. I was scared to death to catch a glimpse of what my hair must look like. Fifteen minutes later, I opened my eyes and he spun me round in the chair to face the mirror. No freaking way! This White dude gave me the second best haircut of my life. Here I was thinking he was a racist skinhead, and this guy had major clipper skills. I couldn't stop shaking his hand and complimenting him on my hair. I tipped him fifty percent because that's all I had.

In this case, trying to avoid sitting in his chair for a haircut wasn't an unconscious bias - I knew exactly what I was doing, stereotyping. The bias was that I equated his color with what I assumed would be his lack of ability to cut a black man's hair, thus leading me to want another black person to cut it. Before he performed his magic and proved me wrong, I would've allowed anyone black to cut my hair before him. I was biased against him due to the belief that Whites knew nothing about my culture or life experiences. Worse, I was biased against his talents because of his demographic makeup. I learned two valuable lessons that day: Taking risks on people's abilities can have great rewards; I had biases that were only revealed under the right circumstances.

There were other times when my biases revealed themselves and embarrassed me to no end. Once I took a flight once from Albany, New York to Boston and had the experience of my life. As we stood patiently waiting (on the runway I might add), this tiny plane rounded the corner and headed in our direction. What the...! Is that? No way! A black dude was behind the controls! It was shocking and funny at the same time. People who had rudely cut in line to board first were suddenly asking, "Would you like to move in front of me?" Nope! You earned your place buddy. Stay right where you are. It was funny until the flight attendant walked up to me and said, "Sir, the pilot wants to know if you would like to be his co-pilot?" Before I could gather my faculties, my mouth spoke up: "I can't. I have to use the bathroom!" My knees were shaking so bad, it looked like I was doing a touchdown celebration. "It's too late, sir, you have to board now." I wobbled into my seat, and the plane was so small, the controls were touching my knees. I was sweating profusely; so much so that the pilot looked at me and asked if I was okay. All I could do was nod and try to keep myself from throwing up. My biases were shouting, "Ask him how long he's been driving the plane?" Yes, I know you don't drive a plane; but my biases against a black dude being in control wouldn't let me say, "fly." I was hoping that all he was going to do was drive up to let us board. Here I am, Mr. Freaking Diversity, and I'm stereotyping this man who looked like me! It was cool to imagine blacks as pilots – right-on, brotha! Do your thing. Yeah, as long as he wasn't doing his thing on the plane I was on. Once we landed, I told him about my S.E.E (significant emotional event). I had to. It was the only therapy I could use to rid myself of the shame and embarrassment I was feeling. We had a good therapeutic laugh and he took a picture with me standing in front of the plane. I asked him to allow my ignorance to fly back with him so he could drop it off over the ocean.

This was the point at which I created a new playbook for myself. The old one was obsolete and could no longer be relied on to help me assess the abilities and skill sets people possess. I was progressing in my careers and becoming more accountable for the productivity of others. If I didn't identify and manage my own biases, they would come back to haunt me. The higher you rise in the ranks, the further you have to fall from grace. Good leaders get the best out of themselves, while great leaders get the best out of others. Getting the best out of people in the workplace without judging them on a personal level takes leadership, not liker-ship. I saw supervisors give people unfavorable performance evaluations based on their biases towards them, and killed the person's career. They would lie about the person's performance and give them a negative evaluation. I'd never seen an evaluation that asked if I liked someone - only how they performed.

The more I taught, the more I saw cracks in the ideology of the ways diversity was being presented. It was about hiring more minorities and more women. We need more diversity of thought! No one talked about biases as one of the biggest barriers to creating diversity, like they are now. Yes, the workplace did and does need all of these things mentioned, but not simply for the sake of having it. These steps must be part of a bigger plan to find talent and use it effectively. In many ways I was learning backwards; first discovering all the things that didn't constitute the concept.

## On the Job Training

While immersed in human relations and diversity training for the military, I served as a recruiting augmenter for my other career with the New York State Police. Since I was both trooper and member of the military, the NYSP thought I was perfect for the job. If it were a horse race, they hit the trifecta. I was a cop, a service member, and black, all in one. After receiving some resistance at my station from one of my bosses who wouldn't allow me to go out and recruit, top leadership intervened on my behalf and transferred me to State Police Headquarters, where I was appointed the Minority Recruiting Coordinator. In this position I traveled to historically black colleges like Spelman and Morehouse College in Atlanta. In between those trips, I hit military installations like Fort Drum Army Post in Watertown, NY, which has a large minority population. It was the first time in my twenty-year career that our organization went to such great lengths to increase its diversity. The number of minority officers in particular was shrinking each year, and there were concerns that the Department of Justice would step in and take action because of it. Minorities were recruited, but they were being disqualified at higher rates than White males. Since the NYSP is a state institution that receives federal funding, the Feds could cut off the cash if we weren't following fair hiring practice guidelines.

Over a two-day recruiting trip to Atlanta, the team and I signed up over a hundred potential candidates for the position of Trooper. All of them were black except for one White guy named Bill Stegner. He was from Upstate New York and heard about our visit on the radio. He told me that he was already a police officer with the Atlanta Police Department, but had always dreamed of being a New York State Trooper. He was one of the people who found themselves stuck on our eligible hire list for three years, and missed out. He sat in the front row and gave us his undivided attention. The session got off to a great start. The audience was filled with young, energetic college students who stumbled over their words from the excitement of having us there. None of them had ever seen a New York State Trooper before and were thrilled we chose their campus to hold the event. Most of the kids were from the inner city, and weren't shy about voicing their opinions. They felt comfortable being real with us, since our team was made up of blacks and Hispanics, like most of them were. We answered their questions honestly, knowing it wouldn't always reflect well on our profession. They asked if we'd ever experienced racism on the job. All of us had, so we answered "yes." We didn't sugarcoat it. Many of them thanked us for not trying to brush over sensitive issues and being honest. Not one person left the room without signing up for the exam.

Here's where the cracks in our recruiting process began to reveal themselves. A twenty-dollar fee was required in order to take the test but before leaving for the trip, our administration said we couldn't accept money from candidates. We were only allowed to collect the names of those who showed interest. The stipulation was if we had enough people signed up, we'd return to Atlanta and give the exam. Only then could we accept money. Anyone who's ever been to college (or who has a child attending school) knows if a student has twenty bucks they're willing to part with, you take it immediately! Money is hard to come by for many students. We were dumbfounded at this decision, since we'd advertised the fee in all of our marketing materials. Many students came with crisp twenty-dollar bills, but we had to tell them to keep the money until we returned. We knew we'd never see those twenties again.

The second problem was that we didn't hold our event until November, just weeks before Thanksgiving. Something strange happens on college campuses between Thanksgiving and New Year's, and it's not Christmas! Many students don't return back to school - not just for a few days, permanently. We generated the interest required for the return trip to administer the exam, but by the time we returned in February, over half the students who signed up in November were no longer there. Worse, we had no way of contacting them. Most of the phone numbers and addresses we'd received were for dorms and apartment complexes the students no longer lived in. On the day of the exam, only twenty-nine out of the original one hundred plus candidates showed up to take the exam. Out of that, only one person scored high enough to be accepted: Bill Stegner, the White dude from New York. We spent all of that money to get a candidate we could've recruited by email. We went to one of the blackest cities in America and came back with a White guy.

Initially, we all felt like this was a catastrophic failure and from an economic standpoint, it was. We didn't accomplish what we set out to do, which was to recruit more minorities. We failed at getting numbers, and we failed economically. One thing we didn't fail at was diversity, because we weren't actually applying it. We were applying Affirmative Action. What the State Police offered was an equal chance to compete for a position without the assurance of an outcome. That's the basis of Affirmative Action: to provide an equal opportunity for employment, and that's it. There are no guarantees that a person will be hired. They're only given an equal chance to apply based on meeting the qualifications of the job.

Since we didn't understand the meaning of diversity, we relied on numbers alone to measure our success the same way diversity was being sold to everyone. Had I known myself, I would've channeled our energy in a different direction. I would've advised our leadership to focus more effort on highlighting and including the women and minority members already in the organization - start by promoting those who'd worked hard and proven themselves to be outstanding Troopers. I knew a few of them, but when it came time for special assignments and promotions they were always passed over. What good is it to collect bodies if they aren't going to be included and acknowledged by the organization? This question led to a third problem I came across. Most of the minority troopers in the organization who had children old enough to be candidates themselves chose not to persuade them to take the entrance exam. When I asked why, every one of them said: "Because I don't want them to go through the harsh treatment that I went through."

*Like many organizations, we looked outside our walls to find diversity instead of cultivating what we already had. Diversity is never achieved through numbers. Members of a diverse group can be counted, but in many cases, the "E" in diverse stands for exclusion. The measures we took were 'affirmative acts' to attract people from underrepresented groups; the core of Affirmative Action. However, taking measures or actions such as hiring, training, creating employee support programs, etc. should never be looked at as the whole of diversity. Actions like these help to create it, but only when employees are truly part of their organization.*

We did get a good trooper in Bill Stegner. A few weeks after we returned from the trip, I was watching an episode of "Cops," and to my surprise, Bill was being highlighted on the show for making a significant drug arrest. He continued working at a high level once he became a New York State Trooper. After about a year, he transferred to the station I worked at, and I became his supervisor.

# 4

# COMPREHENDING THE CONCEPT OF DIVERSITY

## The Bridge to Understanding

If counting minority hires and Affirmative Action weren't diversity, then what was? Better yet, why did we even need it? It seemed as if every time I had breakthrough, another question popped up. I couldn't stop propositioning myself, and I became frustrated with all of it. Doubt started to creep in and I began to think: "Maybe this is some made-up crap to give people reason to make up more crap." (Humans are good at that. We make up some crazy topic then specialize the heck out of it until it means something, which creates a need for experts on it, who fool everyone into thinking that the stuff they're talking about is important.)

It seemed like a simple concept until I became one of the experts I just described. All of a sudden, this thing called diversity had become so important in the workplace that everyone was jumping on the bandwagon. But someone forgot to send the memo out to the employees, advising them that adding women and minorities to the workforce was necessary. No one told them that women and minorities weren't coming to replace them and take their jobs. What they were being told was that Affirmative Action was forcing companies to hire unqualified people to come share the workplace with them. The unqualified part was an exaggeration of the truth because at times this did occur. Many organizations rushed to get numbers so at times candidates weren't properly vetted. However, the part about Affirmative Action forcing companies to hire minorities wasn't. The Federal Government was cracking down on organizations who received federal funding but who weren't actually hiring women and minorities. In turn, organizations kept changing the qualification standards as a way to say they were trying, but couldn't find qualified minorities. It still happens today. Since companies and other organizations had been successful without women and minorities, there wasn't a need to treat them with dignity and respect. Who were these people, to come disrupt the establishment? Diversity as it was being presented didn't mean a thing in the workplace at the time and why should it?

One day, as I was driving through my neighborhood, I noticed a group of kids playing in the road. They didn't notice me or seem to have a care in the world. They were too busy having fun. Once they saw me, they moved aside and waved feverishly with all their little teeth showing. I saw everything they'd eaten for dinner! Juice stains and sauces were smeared all over their clothes and cheeks. I thought to myself, "Just wait 'till you little devils grow up and have to go to work: you won't be smiling so much then." Eureka! That was it! Work! Work itself was the reason the concept of diversity was necessary in America. Seeing kids playing together reminded me of my childhood. Everyone in the neighborhood played together regardless of race, color, or gender. As we got older, that changed. Most of us went our separate ways and formed new friendships; mostly with people from our own race. No one told us we had to. We just did. As we get older, we have tendency to associate with people we share commonalities with. As they say: 'Birds of a feather flock together.' When left to choose most go with what's familiar and comfortable to us.

*The workplace is different. It's the one place in which diverse populations like ours, in America, must congregate to attain the means for survival. Because we live in an advanced society with a constitution, which declares "All persons born or naturalized in this country are citizens of this country," (14th Amendment) America was destined to need the concept of diversity. Everything from our governments to all of our public and private organizations add to the institution called "work." There's no other platform where adult minorities, women, and White males have to formally interact together except at work. America was introduced to the industrial age at the same time slavery was abolished and an influx of Irish, Italian, Jewish, and many other immigrants arrived on its shores. Most people discount these groups as immigrants based on skin color alone, but they made up the majority of immigrants to this country. All of these occurrences made diversity a necessary concept, but no one knew it at the time. From my experience, it doesn't appear that we've learned much about its importance to the workplace. There's more work to do.*

When given the choice, most will choose to engage with members of their own demographic group. It's reflected in the communities we live in, lunchrooms and churches alike. People feel most comfortable around their own. Forcing them to interact with each other requires a purpose, and work is that purpose. We don't have to hunt or scavenge for food anymore. We work so that we can hit the grocery store on the way home. This was the fundamental reason human relations, cultural awareness, and diversity training weren't working. These concepts were being taught as workplace niceties and not workplace necessities. Most of the training focused on equality and treating people fairly. While I understood both of these things were critical to the work environment neither of them illustrated the reason why women and minorities should be in the workplace. Since the importance of their roles was never established, there was no business case for diversity. There was no connection made between demographics and the skill sets needed to make companies profitable. How did they relate to each other? Diversity as it was being presented didn't ensure productivity in for-profit or nonprofit organizations like the military or law enforcement, either. In an advanced society like America, human survival was, and still is, the business case for diversity. We have to work to remain part of the mainstream, and that in itself is survival for most Americans. We don't need cable TV, cell phones, three cars, video games, or social media to survive, but we think we do. Profits, high productivity, loyalty, etc. are the rewards received when diversity is implemented correctly. They aren't the reason for it - survival is.

*Discovering the true reason for diversity made me see it as a workplace necessity. Once slavery was abolished in America and immigrants continued to arrive on our shores, diversity became a workplace requirement. Slaves gave birth to the offspring who sacrificed themselves for civil rights, which included the right to earn a living. These families had to find work to survive, just as Whites did. The industrial age sparked by World Wars I and II required an enormous workforce, and White men couldn't do it alone. There were simply not enough of them to fight the wars and provide the support needed to sustain the battles. While the ideas of White men created the infrastructure for an advanced society, women, minorities, immigrants and Whites all worked together to transform these ideas into reality. This was the precursor for establishing diversity as a workplace necessity.*

## **The Purpose of Diversity**

I discovered the reason for diversity and why it mattered. It mattered because people have to work to survive. As said in the movie Field of Dreams: "If you build it, they will come." America had an ever-increasing diverse population that needed to find work to survive. If there was a business, company, nonprofit organization, or institution, which provided employment, people were going to show up and apply. The concept was needed for one purpose: To help organizations establish a mechanism by which maximum effort and productivity could be achieved by a diverse group of employees who had never worked together before.

## **Components of Diversity, the Functional Equation**

By this time in my careers, I had direct knowledge as to the reasons women and minority employees were leaving the workplace early. They weren't being utilized to their fullest potential and had been excluded from being integrated into the DNA of the organization. No mentorship, no opportunities for career advancement, and alienation were a few of the reasons noted. It was common then (and still is today) for employers to state women leave the workplace to have families and raise children. That's stretching the truth. Some have, but many of them left to pursue opportunities they weren't getting in their jobs. They simply filled "quotas" that organization's first created themselves then blamed the Federal Government for being forced to have. This was another stretch. By law, there was only one group of people at this particular time that could legally be hired using a quota system: those with disabilities. Thanks to President Obama, that has changed. Military veterans have been added to this group with the creation of executive order 13518, which mandates that the federal government hire and retain veterans using a quota system. It ensures every department hires certain numbers of veterans. No other group - not blacks, Hispanics, Asians, Pacific Islanders, women, or our Native Americans - could legally be hired under a quota system. Doing so was and is a violation of law and federal courts would side against an organization for doing it. Even so, organizations used it to stay in favor with the Feds. They didn't want to lose the money the government was giving them to support some of their programs. Civil Rights and Affirmative Action have been around for decades, but many organizations hadn't figured out how to make it work in their best interests. Even if they managed to ensure that women and minorities were hired, it still wouldn't have met the standard for workplace diversity.

## **The Equation**

Looking back at the path of my professional careers, I identified three absolute necessities that must work together to create the synergy necessary for achieving workplace diversity: "Representation + Inclusion + Performance =

Diversity." It's what I termed the "functional equation." It's like a table with three legs: remove one of them, and it will topple over. If organizations couldn't make all three components work together as one, there was no diversity. This principal defined my career paths and why I don't use the phrase "diversity and inclusion." Being selected as an officer in the military and joining Major Brady's staff was the first component of diversity, *"Representation."* I was from an underrepresented group, was qualified, and happened to be only the second black member in my unit's history to move from the enlisted ranks to becoming a commissioned officer. I fulfilled all the requirements and was given an opportunity. I did my part to be ready, and the unit did theirs.

What made me stay in the unit for as long as I did was the second component: the *"Inclusion"* my leaders provided by inviting me to meetings, speaking with me one-on-one, and giving me the mentorship I needed as a first-generation officer. It helped me gain confidence in my work. It also allowed me to see how leaders made decisions, with whom they relied on for information, and how they interacted with each other. I was able to learn the culture. Including me in the everyday activities of the unit (the DNA) was an important step these leaders took in cultivating diversity. It gave me visibility throughout the organization and made my role as the Military Equal Opportunity Officer credible. No longer did people see the office as a dark place, dealing with dark issues concerning dark people. Along with my counterparts and close friends James Hockey and Kristina Blodgett, we legitimized the office and made it an asset for our commanders. Without our Base Commander's efforts to include the office (and me personally) in the fabric of the organization, I can say with confidence that it wouldn't have happened. I discovered through research and the exit interviews I've been a part of, that two of the main reasons minorities and women leave the workplace are isolation and a lack of leadership support. Inclusion is the key. It's the link to getting commitment from employees and stimulates the last component of diversity: "*Performance*."

Due to the fact that the 174th leaders (my unit) took affirmative action by giving me an equal opportunity to be included, I performed well. I gave them everything I had because I was committed to the organization. If my commanders called me while I was out of town or working my civilian job, I made sure to provide them with whatever they needed. If they had told me to go to hell, I would've asked them if they wanted me to kick the devil's butt while I was down there. I spent countless hours of my own time preparing for inspections and teaching required courses for the unit. I made it my mission to provide value to my organization. I studied my craft and become the subject-matter expert in human relations and diversity for the unit. I made myself a valuable asset. I didn't wait for someone to tell me to read the manuals and regulations to learn my profession. I just did it. I used my own time and money, when necessary, to learn my art; and it paid off. This wasn't kissing up to anyone or brown-nosing (as we used to call it back in the day). It's what I call "returning a profit on their investment (ROI)". When organizations establish true diversity, this is the commitment employees will give to their employers.

My leadership didn't put me on the staff simply because of my color or race. To do so would've only required me to sit around and be black all day. If that's all they wanted, then there shouldn't have been any expectation of me to perform. That would've made for an easy career. I'd been black for thirty-eight years, by that time. I'm sure I had the art of blackness mastered already. One of my State Police supervisors once asked why I spent so much of my vacation leave time working for my military unit. My answer was simple: "They never told me no, so I will never tell them no!"

*Getting the best out of people is simple. Show them what you want, include them, then allow and encourage them to participate the best way they know how as long as it's safe, ethical, and productive. It will foster appreciation, which in turn helps to establish employee loyalty to the organization. A colleague once told me: "You don't have to worry about the people who quit and leave the job. You have to worry about the ones who quit and stay (meaning: they'll never perform at their maximum level, and will keep the organization from reaching its full potential). To the contrary: when people from underrepresented groups are welcomed into the organization and included as full-fledged employees, it's likely they will perform at a higher level than expected.*

I'd discovered it - the functional equation, which illustrates just how diversity works. "Representation + Inclusion + Performance = Diversity" formed the foundation for workplace diversity. After analyzing the process by which I had success in my careers, I knew this synergy made it possible. I believe in it so much that later on I went through the painstaking task of having the phrase trademarked. Finally I discovered what I'd been in search of; the true definition of diversity. The feeling of accomplishment rushed through my body like a shot of adrenaline. I stared at each part of the equation for hours, like I'd won the lottery. One by one, I examined the ideas closely, needing to make sure the formula was correct. Then I noticed something. If I removed

"*Inclusion*," I was left with Affirmative Action. If I removed "*Performance*," I was left with what Laura Liswood, author of "The Loudest Duck," refers to as the "Noah's Ark version of diversity": "Give me two blacks, two Hispanics, two women, and two of every other kind, and we have diversity." This happens when people are hired by an organization solely for demographic representation. Without all three components working together to form the framework, workplace diversity doesn't exist. The formula I discovered (*Representation + Inclusion + Performance = Diversity®*) became my brand and the philosophy by which I would forever teach the concept.

*Whenever I see or hear the term "diversity and inclusion," red flags go up. True diversity is inclusive. When it comes to workplace diversity, inclusion can never be connected by the conjunction 'and'. This indicates they can stand alone; one component without the other. They must be connected together to form a greater sum: Representation + Inclusion + Performance = Diversity. When there's no inclusion, you're left with Affirmative Action, which seeks to attract, identify, train, and promote individuals from underrepresented groups in the workplace. Affirmative Action doesn't require acceptance into an organization; nor does it address inclusion into all of its formal and informal functions. These functions include (but are not limited to): meetings, social activities, having lunch together, discussing family or life issues, fostering mutual respect for one another, and sharing valuable work information - actions that signal one's full acceptance into the organization. Inclusion is the most critical component of diversity because the feeling of being accepted most often stimulates maximum employee performance.*

For a young officer like me, having solid support showed that I was appreciated and accepted by my organization. For a young *black* officer, it meant I was valued not just as an officer, but as a man. Going through life feeling that the country I lived in saw my blackness as a threat, the respect my unit gave me offered comfort from the loneliness and alienation I felt at times. I was proud of my accomplishment; but moreover, I was proud that I was fully accepted. I didn't care if I was liked on a personal level. I was recognized for my skills and didn't have to compromise myself. For minorities and women, that means the world. This stood as a model for the way organizations can successfully incorporate diversity. It wasn't about how many minorities we had in the unit - it was more about including minorities in the unit. This was what Dr. Betances meant when he said "Making heads count!"

By no means was my unit free of negative issues like discrimination. Before I joined, it had been hit with a sex discrimination complaint by a female pilot who claimed she was kept from performing special missions by her all-male chain of command. The complaint was substantiated, and the unit was made to remove the tag-line "Boys from Syracuse" from all signage and equipment on the base. It also cost some leaders their careers. These things will happen in organizations; but what's important is how the issues are addressed. In my case, I reaped the benefits of the leadership's efforts to correct a wrong. Diversity isn't perfect: it's a process that works to get us close to perfection. My experience was also an example of diversity management. Including someone like myself, with unique life experiences, allowed my organization to use those experiences and my talents to benefit itself. They put me in a position that played to my strengths and abilities while supporting me all the way through my career. Representation + Inclusion + Performance = Diversity®.

## No Time for Admiration

There was no time to stop and marvel over what I'd discovered. Now came the hard part: I had to figure out how to translate my findings into something that would make sense to people. I was concerned about convincing other practitioners because they have the role of articulating diversity to their organizations. However, I was more interested in connecting with the general public; 'Joe the plumber' types. These were the middle-class White workers who felt they'd been forgotten and that minorities were coming to take their jobs. They were an audience I needed to reach for sure. Since they made up the majority of American employees they would most likely become bosses and leaders of an ever-changing demographic workplace.

But there was also a third group I wanted to reach: the ones who had given up on their dreams - those frustrated by trying to fit into organizations that didn't accept them for one reason or another. Maybe they'd been unfamiliar with the environment, didn't find the work challenging enough, weren't liked by their peers, or just people who were used to fill quotas. Whatever the reason, I had to reach them. I knew that by explaining the concept of diversity in a different manner, I could help them navigate through the workplace better and accomplish their dreams. I could show practitioners and leaders alike how to gain commitment from their employees; not just compliance. Sun Tzu, the great Chinese philosopher, suggested that it's never wise to attempt to win an argument with words, but rather, by actions. It was time for me to show that diversity wasn't simply a tag line for hiring minorities and women, but an active process that required employers to fully engage all of its employees to get the best out of them.

## **When Segregation is Necessary**

The deeper I dove into the concept of diversity the clearer it became that people had been misinformed and misled to believe that Affirmative Action, Equal Employment Opportunity and diversity were all the same thing. People were being taught that organizations should hire based on demographics and should treat these new employees fairly by training, promoting, and celebrating cultural differences, on occasion. The workplace was being used to address social ills like racism and discrimination, which made sense considering both issues disrupted the work environment. The problem was that training was used as the scapegoat for corrective action when instead, disciplinary measures, which drove home a zero tolerance stance on discrimination, harassment, and racism should have been enforced by organizations. That left those who were trying to deliver a message about diversity scrambling to address cultural and racial tensions. The topics of Affirmative Action and Equal Opportunity couldn't be avoided in this case, but it had ill effects. After spending an hour or two arguing over sensitive issues like these, no time was left to talk about the progressive nature required to implement diversity. By then, no one wanted to hear about it, anyway. They were too angry to listen.

The majority group (White men) had no vested interest in distinguishing the differences between these topics. There didn't appear to be anything in it for them. There was no 'WIFM' ("what's in it for me," as we call it in the diversity world). When Major Brady told me at the onset of my career that White males found it difficult to listen to blacks talk about equality and human relations, this is exactly what he was talking about. Why would they listen if they weren't receiving any benefit? Can't say I blame them, though. During the early '90s, human relations and cultural awareness classes were like training for a boxing match, and White guys were the punching bags. They got blamed for more things than President Obama did during his presidency. No one was going to convince them that there was a need for minorities and women in the workplace after being verbally assaulted for half a day in one of these classes. They had to sit and listen to how racist and unfair they'd been, only to have their critics insist they support their diversity efforts. It was like inviting someone to your house for dinner, and after they complained all night about how terrible your food was, had the nerve to ask for desert!

It was important to separate the concepts of Affirmative Action, Equal Opportunity, and diversity because although they may cross paths at times, there's a distinct difference between them. Affirmative Action takes steps to ensure that underrepresented groups are given equal chance to enter the workplace, be trained like everyone else, and have an opportunity for promotions. It doesn't guarantee that a person be hired. It was never designed to do so. Organizations using it as a guaranteed hiring practice for women and minorities were doing it because they lacked the numbers and knew that if they didn't increase them, they stood a chance of losing federal funding. They wouldn't tell White applicants the real reason minorities were being selected over them. According to the many White males I've spoken to over the years, when they were turned down for employment, the hiring agent would say: "Sorry - if you aren't black or female, we can't hire you. We have to take them first." I'm sure that was true and probably happened exactly the way they told me, but there was more to the story.

They were never told that, for years, qualified minorities and women had been passed over and now it has come back to haunt the organization. From the White male perspective, there wasn't any equality. They felt now they were the ones being discriminated against.

As for Equal Opportunity programs, they were created out of a need to address the unlawful discrimination and disparaging treatment women and minorities faced as a result of coming into the workplace. Its relevance to diversity was simple: without fair and equitable treatment, diversity as a workplace concept couldn't survive. You would never get full commitment from these groups - they'd pack up and leave. It was the safety mechanism used to protect the rights of people to work in a harassment-free environment. Unfortunately in most cases it didn't work. People figured out how to get around it. If everyone in an office denied that an individual was being discriminated against, an allegation was difficult to prove. When there's sufficient evidence to show that discrimination did, in fact, occur, the agency or organization would sweep the matter under the rug and go back to business as usual. In many cases, the complainant would be fired or ostracized to the point where they'd give up and leave.

Diversity is about utilizing talents, incorporating skill sets, and including the ideas of all employees in spite of cultural, ethnic, gender identity, or other individual differences. I say 'in spite of ' because those are the characteristics that often keep people from being hired in the first place. It's the concept that keeps employees from walking out the door. Diversity can't be counted unless the idea is to only have quantitative information. Diversity as a workplace concept should be measured for its effectiveness.

To want a diverse workforce is good, but the question is for what, to sit around and count the number of minorities and women in workplace or to use their life experiences and abilities to create a more productive organization? The reason matters; absolutely! It will dictate how people will or will not be included in the work environment. The concept is more than assembling a diverse group of people together in the workplace. It's about getting the best out of their unique abilities.

*You don't get diversity as it pertains to the workplace simply by having a diverse group of people or making laws to protect them. If they can't work together, be productive together, accomplish goals and tasks together, and, more importantly, profit because of it, then diversity doesn't and can't exist. Diversity is not what you begin with; it's what you end up with once you have a diverse workforce that works together effectively. It's about incorporating the skills and abilities of people in spite of demographics; not because of them. If it were practiced this way, it wouldn't matter who was hired to do a job as long as they were competent and utilized their skills to better the organization.*

## **When Not to Follow the Leader**

Just as there was a need to distinguish the differences between concepts, there was a time to break away from some terms I felt were overly used and exaggerated; the first being "Best Practices." In this case, I had to be analytical, since I wanted the concept of diversity and diversity training to be taken seriously. A *'best practice'* is a process or method that's become a standard in a particular industry because it's been proven over time to be superior over every other process or method previously used. First, there's neither been an industry standard established for incorporating diversity into an organization, nor one established for how to conduct diversity training. Second: what worked for one organization, may be completely inappropriate for another - therefore, how could one practice be seen as 'best'?

If the term "best practices" were used to describe principles that've been tested over time and proven to be effective by the "majority" of professionals in the field, I wouldn't have much gripe. Techniques such as taking measures to avoid attacking your audience on a personal level or purposely embarrassing someone are examples of practices that the majority of instructors, trainers, and public speakers would agree on without much debate. However, when the term "best" is used to describe diversity strategies that have only achieved small results, I start to cringe. It's an unnecessary exaggeration that, when tested, won't stand up to criticism.

Some of my colleagues get upset with me for being so critical about this, but it's really not my fault. I was born with a skepticism gene that often got me into trouble growing up. Whenever my mother threatened to do bodily harm to me for misbehaving, she'd say: "Boy, if you keep it up, I'm going to knock you into the middle of next week!" I thought, "If you could do that, why not hit me hard enough to get me to the weekend, then I wouldn't have to go to school?" Once, I decided to present this thought to her, which turned out to be a bad idea. By the time she finished with me, I was convinced that if she couldn't knock me into the weekend, she could at least whip me until it came. Thankfully, it didn't kill my inquisitive spirit, because this characteristic came in handy, as a law enforcement officer. It helped me solve some of the cases I investigated by critically analyzing and questioning statements and clues.

My concern about phrases like *best practices* is that they discredit the profession by making weak claims that don't rise to the level of "best." I'm not a researcher by trade, but after performing research at the Master's Degree level, I developed a healthy respect for the amount of work that goes into proving *good* practices, let alone 'best.' A program doesn't need a title like 'best' in order to be effective. It simply needs to work. In this case, a good training program that continues to evolve and gets better over time is what I look for. Unless it's tested in multiple arenas, for multiple years, and proven to be better than all other training, it's not the best, and doesn't need to be. It just needs to work. Clichés like this are a sign of laziness, and lack critical thinking. Whenever I hear over-exaggerated terms, it becomes difficult for me to take the topic seriously. I wanted to be credible and have the topic of diversity taken seriously. To accomplish both, I'd have to address the weaknesses in the concept and change the way people perceived it. If diversity couldn't move beyond demographic categories and clichés, eventually it would fade away. My job was to keep breathing life into it until my apprenticeship was complete.

# 5

# PERSONAL CONTRIBUTION

## Diversity and Self Awareness

Diversity was introducing me to this new person I was evolving into. I learned that I was sensitive to other people's pain and hated to argue, but loved intellectual debate. I wasn't concerned with being famous, but admired those who could handle it. I loved to landscape, plant flowers, and proud of it. I feared failure more than anything. Seeing elderly couples out for a Sunday drive in their antique cars brought me joy, and I had the highest admiration for renaissance people and finely-tailored suits. Even though I'm a total Ice Cube fan, I'd argue that Freddie Mercury of Queen was one of the greatest entertainers of all time. I'd never assessed my personal catalog before; once I did, I was surprised at what I found out about myself. The process gave me the insight to fully appreciate myself as a person and showed I was just as weird, just as simple, and just as complex as anyone else. I could use all of my skill sets to forge my own path as long as I was willing to deal with some hell from time to time, and not get sidetracked. I was naive enough to think I could make a difference, hard-headed enough to keep trying to learn in spite of distractions, and wise enough to know that I didn't know everything. I stopped focusing on what others had, like opportunities, titles, lifestyle, etc. I realized that those things were theirs, and I had no right of ownership to any of it. They had their journey, just as I had mine. Quite simply: I had power - power over my actions. That was enough for me. I had all I needed to keep me headed in the direction of understanding and redefining diversity. My needs for this journey were met. I didn't want anything else except a complete understanding of what I was putting together. In that state of being, I could concentrate on mastering my art.

Abraham Maslow, an American psychologist best known for creating the Hierarchy of Needs Motivational Theory, asserted that while people aim to fulfill basic needs such as food, water, and shelter, they also seek to meet higher needs. At the top of his scale is self-actualization, which refers to the need for personal growth and discovery that's present in a person's life. He cited there were a number of needs that must be met before pursuing other ones. He suggested physiological safety, love/belonging, and esteem, had to be met first in order to achieve self-actualization. Two key characteristics of this level are lack of prejudice and acceptance of facts. Once I discovered I had privileges that I deeply appreciated, it was easier for me to see why the dominant group wouldn't want to give theirs up. I found I also had privileges that I didn't earn. I was born into them by arriving on this planet as a man. These were the facts. Acknowledging that my own privileges as a man were at the expense of women was a fact I'd have to accept, but it was only possible once I was good with who I was as a person.

*Self-actualization is further described this way:*

**Acceptance and Realism:** *Self-actualized people have realistic perceptions of themselves, others, and the world around them.*

**Problem Centering:** *Self-actualized individuals are concerned with solving problems outside of themselves, including helping others and finding solutions to problems in the external world. These people are often motivated by a sense of personal responsibility and ethics.*

**Spontaneity:** *Self-actualized people are spontaneous in their internal thoughts and outward behavior. While they can conform to rules and social expectations, they also tend to be open and unconventional.*

**Autonomy and Solitude:** *Another characteristic of self-actualized people is the need for independence and privacy. While they enjoy the company of others, these individuals need time to focus on developing their own individual potential.*

**Continued Freshness of Appreciation:** *Self-actualized people tend to view the world with a continual sense of appreciation, wonder, and awe. Even simple experiences continue to be a source of inspiration and pleasure.*

Self-Actualization, as I learned, wasn't about money or the accomplishments one may achieve. I knew plenty of wealthy people who were never satisfied with their success in spite of having all the material trappings in the world. They weren't content. They needed constant praise and would crush anyone who didn't bow down or give them what they wanted. On the flip side, I've met people who didn't have cable TV, never owned a car less than ten years old, and never had the corner office with the five-thousand-pound maple desk and high-back chair, but were the happiest people in the entire building. They didn't need fame or fortune to be content and didn't seem to care what people thought of them. They just worked hard and provided for their families. If I wasn't good with myself, it would keep me from delivering an impartial message. I'd take the liberty of directing personal jabs at anyone who crossed me the wrong way. My concerns would be limited to things that hurt me in the past, and my hunger to be better than everyone else would supersede my mission to present diversity correctly.

> On my journey to discovering diversity, I found more than I was looking for. I found that I was happy with myself. I was flawed as a man, but perfect in my own way; stubborn at times, yet compassionate towards the needs of others. None of it mattered though. Diversity was the only thing that made any difference to me outside of my family, and I felt responsible for finding its true meaning. It was mine and no one else's. The search for it made me take an honest assessment of myself and the life I was living. Once I did, I approved of it all. I didn't need to be the smartest person in the room, didn't need to be rich, didn't need to be the man on the streets, I just needed to find the meaning of diversity and how to use it. This made me ok with any shortcomings I had. The assessment brought clarity as to why I had certain weakness and strengths. I'm human - I'm supposed to have both. All that meant was that I needed others to make up for my weaknesses; and in return, I could use my strengths to make up for theirs. In that respect, I could work smarter, not harder. The reality is: none of us are as complete by ourselves as we are with others who complement our talents and skill sets. Once I became aware of that, I was good with who I was and could remain focused on my mission.

## **Mastering the Art**

Enlightened by self-awareness, I turned my attention to working on delivery. It was equally as important to master the art of presentation, as it was to have sound, solid material. I couldn't afford to miss a beat on anything. From what Major Brady told me and from what I'd witnessed from my own experiences, the topic of diversity didn't receive warm welcomes. If my material couldn't change minds or challenge perceptions my presentation style would have to. I'd have to be outstanding every time I stepped on stage.

In his book *Mastery,* Robert Greene describes the path by which highly acclaimed author Zora Neale Hurston (1891-1960) mastered the art of writing. As Greene describes it, there is an apprenticeship stage that one must go through in order to gain the depth of knowledge required for mastery. This is how he explains it:

*Zora Neale Hurston's story reveals in its barest form the reality of the Apprenticeship Phase - no one is really going to help you or give you direction. In fact, the odds are against you. If you desire an apprenticeship, if you are to learn and set yourself up for mastery, you have to do it yourself and with great energy. When you enter this phase, you generally begin at the lowest position. Your access to knowledge and people is limited to your status. If you are not careful, you will accept this status and become defined by it, particularly if you come from a disadvantaged background. Instead, you must struggle against any limitations and continually work to expand your horizons. (In each learning situation you will submit to reality, but that reality does not mean you must stay in one place.) Reading books and materials that go far beyond what is required is always a good starting point. Being exposed to ideas in the wide world, you will tend to develop a hunger for more and more knowledge; you will find it harder to remain satisfied in any narrow corner, which is precisely the point. The people in your field, in your immediate circle, are like worlds unto themselves-their stories and viewpoints will naturally expand your horizons and build up your social skills. Mingle with as many different types of people as possible. Those circles will slowly widen. Any kind of outside schooling will add to the dynamic. Be relentless in your pursuit for expansion. Whenever you feel like you are settling into some circle, force yourself to shake things up and look for new challenges, as Hurston did when she left Howard for Harlem. With your mind expanding, you will redefine the limits of your apparent world. Soon, ideas and opportunities will come to you and your apprenticeship will naturally progress.*

Having two careers at the same time gave me the opportunity to expand my horizons just as Hurst did. Since I was one of few minorities in both workplaces, the process of going outside of my normal comfort zone was automatically created for me. I dove in headfirst. I talked to anything and anyone that had a pulse. It wasn't an easy transition for me, at first. I'm an introvert by nature, and like my privacy. I wasn't accustomed to walking up to strangers and striking up conversations - it's awkward. I noticed that whenever someone approached me, though, I could roll with it easily and talk their ears off. Therefore, I had to master another technique called 'smiling'. It's free, easy to accomplish, and goes a long way. I wish I had discovered it before having those conversations with the mirror years ago; it would've spared me some heartache.

My mission was to understand people not only individually, but as a society. I wanted to converse with them, so I used my smile to open the door. I needed to know what attracts humans to each other, their belief systems, likes and dislikes. The more I conversed with people outside my demographic group, the more I noticed that our life experiences are what make us different from one another. Color, race, and gender make us different physically, but the way we are treated because of those traits makes our experiences a much greater factor in determining how we act. Once I discovered how influential experiences were to personal development, I started allowing myself to have more awkward moments by initiating dialogue. I would listen to conversations around me and time my entry. Sometimes it only took eye contact and a smile; other times it was a chuckle at a comment I overheard. The intent was to give myself as many experiences as possible to become a better-rounded person, with depth and insight.

Forcing myself to open up this way gave me a secondary gift. It showed me how to connect with people on their terms. By listening for the right moment to engage, I learned about mannerisms, non-verbal cues, body language, and perceptions. These would become valuable tools for connecting with audiences during training sessions. Mastering the ability to pick up on these cues keyed me in on when to emphasize certain points or when to simply shut up. Silence can be an amazing attention-getter when timed properly. I kept pushing the limits, visiting different countries on my own and trying to speak their language. I never mastered any of them, including Spanish, which I took as a class for four years in high school. But nonetheless, it was an important experience because I became a little more familiar with other cultures. There's nothing like being in a foreign country alone, unable to speak the language. Luckily, in places like Brazil, I blended in and most people thought I was one of theirs. Once I embarrassed myself enough by stumbling over the words, the gig was up, and they knew I was a foreigner. But everyone I met went out of his or her way to help me communicate.

Going to Norway was another great cultural experience. I was the only black person in a sea of White-skinned people, and didn't have any frame of reference to help me with their language. Luckily, most people spoke English as a second or third language, so I was okay most of the time. The funny thing is, due to my skin color, I was treated like royalty. That was an eye-opener! I learned more about black culture there than I had learned at any time in America. I'm not talking about the stuff our country sells us on what it is to be black. I'm talking about real history. It's the place where I first heard of Alexander Pushkin, a black poet who was born in Russia. He's considered by many to be the father of modern Russian literature and was widely acclaimed for his poetry. A real black Russian! Up till then, I only knew of a black Russian as a mixed drink made from five parts vodka to two parts coffee. I had some great experiences there, which I will discuss later in the book. The point here is that pushing myself outside my comfort zone gave me the apprenticeship I needed to understand human relations and begin to shape the way I understood and presented diversity.

### **Fighting Resentment**

Mastering my craft took some anger management to stay focused on what I was trying to achieve. It would have been all too easy for my thoughts to be clouded with anger by revisiting slavery, police brutality, or recalling the first time my son came home crying after someone, whom he thought was a friend, called him a nigger. But to experience diversity for all of its worth required propelling myself away from the trap of collective negativity. I couldn't allow every social issue that affected me as a black man, throw me off course. Searching for the truth forced me to prioritize my energy. I could either spend time being angry at the world, or buckle my chinstrap and grind my way to success. If I allowed anger to take over my soul, I would never be able to recognize people for who they truly are and what they bring to the table.

As a black man in America, there are always distractions, which can throw you off your game. One of them is learning how to survive in a country that sees blackness as evil. Waking up every day only to hear that another unarmed black person was shot and killed by police, or seeing men who look like me being portrayed as pimps, drug dealers, or some deranged character on TV, were the norm. All of this before starting your day, I might add. It's what blacks deal with on a daily basis. It's as common as getting dressed in the morning. We deal with it and keep pushing.

If I allowed these things to overwhelm me, my emotions would highjack my concentration and I wouldn't have been able to recognize people for the talents and skill sets they possess. I would've forever seen them the way I saw Mr. Brady during the human relations class he taught: in a box, doing what my stereotypical point of view said he should be doing - White guy stuff like banking, accounting, science, land development, logistics - anything other than teaching equal opportunity and human relations. I needed laser beam focus to gain a deeper knowledge of diversity, and nothing was going to prevent me from doing it. I expelled the anger and resentment inside me with great force and put myself as close to the experiences of others as I possibly could.

GARY RICHARDSON

# PART 2

# 6

## PREPARATION IS TOUGHER THAN THE GAME

### Time for Action

By 2010, I'd spent a decade grinding it out on the diversity scene. Any opportunity to teach I took. The military provided me with a practice field to hone my skills as a trainer in a formal setting. For two consecutive days each month, I stood before audiences of different ranks, genders, races, religions and ethnicities, presenting my brand of diversity. Prior to 2010, the military and Department of Defense didn't have much guidance on what diversity was, so I was able to explore things my way. I had plenty of time to revamp, restructure, update, or change my training any way I saw fit. I worked feverishly without intervention from the outside world. No one truly cared about diversity in the sense that it was a workplace necessity, but everyone from the military to the business world was being told they had to conduct diversity training. No one knew who was pushing the agenda, because unlike Affirmative Action and equal opportunity, diversity wasn't (and still isn't) mandated by any state or federal laws. Everyone thought it was, though. This misinformation was great for me. I didn't have to force the subject on my military leaders. They assumed we needed it, and we did.

Between the monthly classes I taught at the base, opportunities outside the military came my way. They weren't all based on diversity, but nonetheless, were important to the art of public speaking. I would take any engagement during those days. I wanted more practice to perfect my skills as a speaker. If I were asked to speak at a baking competition, I'd do it! For free if I had to. In fact, I didn't get paid for most of the requests I received prior to 2010, but I didn't care. It gave me face time, and people were beginning to recognize me as a speaker. When I earned my Bachelor's Degree from Empire State College in upstate New York, I was given the honor of speaking for my graduation ceremony. This is when I realized that bigger things were yet to come. I was being forged into a speaker for the specific purpose of delivering diversity to the masses. It wasn't by chance. Too many things occurred which were directly related to me arriving at the point where I was. The Christmas and Easter speeches my parents made me perform in church, me opening my mouth in Mr. Brady's human relations class, having two careers, even playing football in college - all prepared me for teaching diversity. They each conditioned me in unique ways and gave me a repertoire of tools to use for presenting information in a memorable way.

Research suggests that public speaking is one of the single greatest fears people have. Not for me: playing football helped me to perform in spite of fear. My position was running- back, and since I carried the ball it made me a target for opposing teams. To knock a running- back out of the game by smashing into him at full speed was the Holy Grail. Being tackled by guys that weighed a hundred pounds more than me intent on taking my head off made me mentally and physically tough. It took both of these attributes to be a good speaker. You can't allow the size of an audience or their hostility intimidate you, or it will reflect in your confidence to speak and will impact your performance. Being physically fit helps to maintain positive energy throughout a presentation. It's certainly needed during diversity training, because it comes with many challenges. All of my experiences were part of a bigger picture I'd been contracted to paint. Diversity was my Sistine Chapel, my Mona Lisa, my art.

## **Do's and Don't's of Delivering Training**

Practice makes perfect, and there are plenty of missteps along the way. The key is to never stop pursuing your goal no matter how many mistakes are made. On his way to inventing the light bulb, it was said that Thomas Edison made one thousand unsuccessful attempts. When a reporter asked, "How did it feel to fail one thousand times?" Edison replied, "I didn't fail a thousand times. The light bulb was an invention with a thousand steps. *Representation + Inclusion + Performance = Diversity* was a process that took me on a journey of a thousand personal steps before I was enlightened. I definitely fell short on a few occasions, but that was part of the process of learning how diversity works.

Diversity training is much different than any other training I experienced. There were no technical manuals to refer to, like there are in other professions. When I first went into the Air Force, I worked in sheet metal fabrications. Every task had a manual describing the process and steps to take in order to complete it. We were even instructed on which tools to use and given specific safety precautions to ensure that no one got injured. Nothing like that existed for diversity training. You either got it right or suffered the consequences. Although we've had a few decades to perfect the art, there weren't any how-to guides I felt comfortable enough to implement as doctrine. Therefore, I had to learn the hard way.

When I was selected as the Program Manager of the Senior Leadership Team Awareness Seminar, one of my lead instructors decided to welcome me aboard with a little initiation. The seminar is a five-day course composed of several subjects such as socialization, communication across differences, Individual and institutional discrimination, and the prevention of sexual harassment, to name a few. I was responsible for teaching the capstone class titled "Capitalizing on Diversity." The night before, my senior instructor, (who, prior to me joining the team was responsible for teaching diversity) suggested I use a video titled "The Race." He explained how effective it was at stimulating dialog amongst the class. It depicted real-life scenarios using a footrace run by cartoon characters. "This may be Interesting," I thought as I recalled the childhood story about the tortoise and the hare, where the much slower tortoise was victorious by staying diligent and outsmarting his much faster competitor. I asked him to show me the video so I could assess it for myself. It was an eight-minute video depicting three runners: a White male, a female, and a black male, in a race to succeed in life. Along the way, the female and black male competitors ran into numerous obstacles that impeded their progress to succeed. The White male was shown to run freely without anything hindering his progress. He won the race. There were no words spoken by the competitors, no moderator, and no narration; just the race.

After watching it, I agreed it would create dialogue, especially if the class wasn't enthusiastic by then. The instructor smiled at me and said, "This is going to be good." If that wasn't enough, I should've had a clue the next day when I started the video. Suddenly, all the instructors left the classroom like they'd received a hurricane warning. The class started like this: "Hello, my name is Gary Richardson and I'm the Program Manager for the Seminar." I followed up by giving my credentials, and said: "I want to begin the class by showing you a short video called 'The Race.' Please take notes on what you see, and we'll have a discussion about it afterwards." We had a discussion, all right! Once the video ended, the class needed no prompting to engage in dialogue. One student shouted out: "Mr. Richardson what does the video have to do with diversity?" Before I could answer, another said: "I thought we were supposed to be learning how to move forward. This seems to me like it digs up the past and throws it in White males' faces." The entire mood went from being fired up and eager to learn to be ablaze and ready to riot. The black students were just as aroused as the White males who were protesting about what they'd just watched. One black male shouted across the room: "Don't be mad! This is what we go through every day. All you guys did was watch a video; but for us, it's real life."

I wanted dialogue, but this wasn't what I was hoping for - at least, not for a class on diversity. I was hoping the class would acknowledge that the video reflected real life situations and come up with solutions to fix some of the issues. That was expecting too much. I was relying on the students to emotionally decipher the difference between discrimination and diversity when, in reality, that was my job to facilitate not theirs. For the next thirty minutes, I put in some serious work trying to calm the class down and refocus on diversity. It was like watching a tennis match with two John McEnroe's playing against each other; one White and the other black, with me stuck in the middle as the line judge. Finally I was able to gain control over the class by explaining that the video was a "barrier" to embracing diversity because people experience discrimination from different perspectives. It was a true statement, but it wasn't my intent in showing the video. It was a lesson I was learning in real-time. I gave them a ten-minute break and my senior instructor walked into the classroom with a smile on his face and said, "Masterful, Sir. That was awesome. Welcome to the team." I found out he was watching me the entire time from the control room, which is equipped with television monitors that observe every class. Luckily, the block of instruction was two and a half hours long. I had the next seventy minutes to repair the damage.

One mistake in showing the video was that I wasn't aware that a few of the students were sent to the course as a form of punishment. They'd been accused of discriminating against some of their subordinates in their organizations. It's never good to send people to diversity training as a form of punishment. It's like sending a child to church as punishment and then expecting them to see religion as something positive. Participants who are forced to attend courses after being accused of discrimination bring anger and negative energy with them. In most cases, they haven't been enlightened on how their actions affect their ability to lead diverse groups. Had I known this bit of information prior to the class, I would've addressed those issues first. Up to this point, we managed to squash any negative expectations they had concerning the course. We'd turn naysayers into unintentional advocates by stimulating them with new perspectives on human relations. Since the course was designed to foster teamwork and appreciation for the unique talents of others, I should have omitted the video and continued to acknowledge the positive steps organizations have made towards workplace equality. Instead, I took the class back to a dark place filled with anger and resentment. To add, we have a separate class within the training that deals specifically with individual and institutional discrimination, there was no need to revisit it without showing how it relates to diversity. Eventually I showed the connection; but it wasn't planned that way. I believe my instructor suggested using the video to see if the reaction from the students would be the same as when he presented it during a previous class. He got his answer: Yes! He also wanted to see how I'd work myself out of the mess it created. He got that, too. It took valuable time away from the class, which could've been used to move in a positive direction.

*This was a great lesson I learned about teaching diversity: it deserves a stage of its own and shouldn't be mixed in with other topics for shock value. If other topics relate to the subject, by all means, include them; but they should be thoroughly planned and thought out so that they move people forward. The topic of diversity alone will stimulate heated conversations that must be managed correctly to keep participants focused on the bottom line -*

*performance! Don't be afraid to challenge perceptions. There are times when it is absolutely necessary.*

For instance, I've often heard participants use the term 'reverse discrimination' when describing their experience of not being selected over a minority for a job. Courts have used the term in this fashion when a White student or employee files a lawsuit based on discrimination. Unfortunately, there is no such thing. Discrimination is discrimination. I advise people who use this term freely to stop and think for a moment. In order for something to be reversed, it must move in the opposite direction from where it's traveling or where it's pointing. By stating that discrimination has been reversed, you've acknowledged discrimination originally pointed somewhere else. The question is: "When the bus of discrimination was rolling towards everyone else, were you complaining, then?" Because I respected the platform I was given, I took a personal oath to never use it as my personal soapbox for getting back at White people for the pain and anger I've felt over racism and discrimination. Being in a position to speak to audiences is a gift and I vowed to never abuse the privilege. The message I was sending was bigger than me. I was just a vessel to present it. Racism and discrimination are sensitive topics that take time and expertise to explain in a manner, which fosters positive change. These subjects must be acknowledged, but a diversity class, which only lasts for a few hours doesn't offer sufficient time to deal with the emotional struggles people have concerning these issues. I'm not suggesting that training should be watered down so as not to offend anyone. Some people walk in the door offended because they don't believe in equality and don't want to be in the training. What I'm saying is if racism and discrimination must be discussed, have the time it requires to do it justice. Just don't speak on these topics and call it diversity training because it's not. They're barriers to it.

## **Making Training Relative**

What I wanted more than anything was to explain diversity in a way that made people hungry to learn more. Since I realized my experiences meant more to the workplace than my race or color, I'd need to change the mindsets of people about what diversity stood for and how it worked. Attempting to make people share in the experiences of blacks and other minorities wasn't working. I needed to show the advantages of having a diverse workforce and give the listener something tangible to relate to. I couldn't just show statistics. Half the people probably wouldn't believe them and the other half could care less. What I could show them was how I used diversity to achieve my own level of success, both personally and professionally. By this time, I accomplished a few of my long-term goals and was beginning to be recognized for my work in the field of diversity and Military Equal Opportunity. I knew this would be tricky because if I didn't present myself well, I could come off as self-promoting. I've witnessed presenter's give their credentials, only to have someone in the audience feel like they were boasting. There's envy everywhere, no matter what the subject. Misrepresenting diversity was a bigger concern than the criticism though. If stating my accomplishments as a result of learning what diversity was and how to use it was going to be offensive, I was willing to take one for the team.

When I thought back to my upbringing, I remembered my parents impressing upon me and my sibling's ideas like being the best people we could possibly be; saving money for rainy days; paying our bills on time; getting a good education; and working hard. It reminded me that there was a process to living a fulfilled life, whatever that means to each of us as human beings. It may be different for all of us; but nonetheless, there is still a process to make it happen. Mine was to listen to everything my parents said and do seventy-five percent of it, about fifty percent of the time. That way, I allowed myself some time to have fun. I'm sure my parents appreciated my efforts to keep their parenting skills sharpened. I certainly gave them several opportunities. From my perspective, diversity is similar to living a fulfilled life. It required the right pieces, linked together in proper sequence, to make it work. It's not perfect, will come with disappointing moments, and will sometimes be downright confusing. However, once you look back from where you first started, you will have moved a long way towards your goals.

I'd found the pieces to my puzzle. Now it was time to illustrate how they worked together and present it to the masses. The process of incorporating differences for the purpose of accomplishing a goal, mission, or task seemed to be a simple concept. The problem was not many people saw it that way. Those who opposed diversity saw it as a way to take power from one group and give it to another. It was frustrating to think that fear and anger were barriers to something that could do so much good for business, the country, and personal growth. But that's the way it was and to a large extent, still is.

As I stated earlier, I identified three groups of people I really wanted to reach: Practitioners, Joe the Plumber types, and those who'd given up on their dreams. There are a lot of people in these groups, and they are the worker bees - the apprentices, supervisors, and middle managers that will eventually become the leaders of their organizations. I had to connect with them because if I could, they would carry the message forward and spread the word. If I could show them how diversity made an impact on my personal and professional life, maybe they would embrace it. I looked for examples of how diversity created opportunities in spite of failure and disappointment. One thing I knew was that most people aspired to be something special at least once in their lives. Maybe they wanted to become doctors, firefighters, nurses, farmers, or just live a good life. However, something deterred them. I searched for examples of diversity that people could relate to restore their hope.

One of the greatest examples came by way of my late brother, Andre. Growing up in the '70s, I was what was known as a 'latchkey kid'. My parents went to work early in the mornings leaving my siblings and me responsible for getting ourselves off to school. I was the youngest of four boys and attended the afternoon kindergarten class. Since my brothers were older and had to catch the bus, I was last to leave the house. At five years old, I was responsible for making sure my chores were done and the door was locked on my way out. Oh, and I wore the house key around my neck, hence latchkey kid. Andre, my second oldest brother, was a beautiful young man who struggled with drugs and alcohol all his life. He was tall and dark-skinned with perfect, jet-black hair. Whenever he'd blow it out (*a technique used in those days to pull the natural kinks out of hair with a hot straightening comb),* his Afro swayed back and forth like the mane of a lion when it runs. He wasn't a jock like the rest of us, and hated school. He said it bored him, and the teachers were stupid. My poor mother was constantly picking him up after he managed to get suspended for acting out. Once he tricked her into taking care of his marijuana plant by telling her that he was working on a school project, which required him to grow a plant under fluorescent lights in the basement.

She was so proud of him for finally doing his schoolwork. That was until she saw a Cheech and Chong tee shirt with a marijuana leaf on it. I believe she'd still be whipping him to this day if he were still here.

One day after arriving home from school, I heard a sound that changed my life; the way I saw myself, and my abilities. It sounded like a guitar, but I'd never heard one being played that way. Andre received one for Christmas and always tried to mimic a new tune. I thought there was no way he could be playing like that. The windows on the house rattled from the bass coming out of the two-thousand-pound floor model stereo we had. The vibration from those things could shatter glass. (People actually removed the speakers and put them in their cars. They were the first custom car stereos known to mankind.) I wasn't sure if I liked this strange, ground-shaking music, but I couldn't stop listening, frozen in my tracks for fear I'd miss one of those crazy riffs. When the music stopped, I walked in to see Andre sitting on our worn-out blue sofa with his red, black, and yellow electric guitar. He had this smile on his face like he just gotten back from Cedar Point, our favorite amusement park in Ohio. Andre spent a lot of time in the amusement park of his mind (the kind that makes people see unicorns and leaves them with the munchies). I asked him, "Why are you listening to that kind of music? Isn't it for White people?" With eyes glowing like red starbursts, he looked at me and said: "He ain't White." "Yes, he is," I shouted, without even knowing who "he" was. "Who is it then?" I asked. "That's Jimi, man. Jimi Hendrix, the baddest guitar player on earth."

Andre unplugged his guitar and walked over to the mammoth-sized record player. He reached inside the storage area and pulled out a psychedelic album cover. It was the coolest and strangest thing I'd ever seen. It opened the lid to freethinking and allowed me to dream differently. The door that blocked my ambitions of one day becoming something other than a professional athlete or entertainer suddenly disappeared. Jimi was an entertainer himself, but I saw him as a superhero that was unafraid to challenge the evil villain called 'status quo.' Here was this black guy sporting a huge Afro and wearing funky, colorful clothes that looked like something from Ringling Brothers and Barnum Bailey Circus! I couldn't take my eyes off of him. Who was he? What made him play this wild rock music, and who the hell taught him to make the guitar wail like that? This wasn't normal for a black guy. We played rhythm and blues, jazz, or gospel music. I needed to find out more about this Jimi dude.

 I searched for any information I could find about Mr. Hendrix. It wasn't the age of the Internet, yet, so word of mouth and various pop culture magazines were all I had to go on. I couldn't find much at the time, but the intrigue stayed with me. I bought several of his CDs over the years and listened to them over and over again. In 1995, I went on a two-week annual tour to Norway with the $105^{th}$ Air National Guard unit out of Newburgh, New York. One day, during breakfast, I met a sweet, elderly Norwegian woman who'd worked at the dining hall for several years. She was floored to meet a black person from the States. I was the only person of color on the trip with my unit, and the fact that we were from New York only added to her excitement. We talked about everything, including music. I was surprised at the wealth of knowledge she had about black artists. She mentioned everyone from an old gospel group my parents often talked about, "The Five Blind Boys," to R&B icon Keith Sweat. Then she hit the jackpot when she mentioned Jimi Hendrix! She told me that back in the early '50s and '60s, many black artists came to Europe to launch their careers, and Jimi was one of them. She advised me to visit any of the music stores in town and I'd see all of his music on display. I took her up on it; and boy, was she telling the truth. What I found most amazing was how highly he was regarded by greats like Paul McCartney, Bob Dylan and Eric Clapton. They called him the greatest guitar player in the world. Here's what Rolling Stone Magazine had to say about him:

*Hailed by Rolling Stone as the greatest guitarist of all time, Jimi Hendrix was also one of the biggest cultural figures of the Sixties, a psychedelic voodoo child who spewed clouds of distortion and pot smoke.*

*A left-hander who took a right-handed Fender Stratocaster and played it upside down, Hendrix pioneered the use of the instrument as an electronic sound source. Players before Hendrix had experimented with feedback and distortion, but he turned those effects and others into a controlled, fluid vocabulary every bit as personal as the blues with which he began.*

*Born November 27, 1942, in Seattle, Washington, Hendrix taught himself to play guitar as a teenager, listening to records by blues guitarists Muddy Waters and B.B. King and rockers such as Chuck Berry and Eddie Cochran. He played in high school bands before enlisting in the U.S. Army in 1959. Discharged in 1961, Hendrix began working under the pseudonym Jimmy James as a pickup guitarist. By 1964, when he moved to New York, he had played behind Sam Cooke, B.B. King, Little Richard, Jackie Wilson, Ike and Tina Turner, and Wilson Pickett. In New York he played the club circuit with King Curtis, the Isley Brothers, John Paul Hammond, and Curtis Knight.*

It was astonishing to see this! Here was this black guy, playing hard-core rock during the turbulent '60s. We're talking about the same time that black civil rights leaders like Dr. Martin Luther King Jr., Malcolm X, and Medgar Evans were assassinated. President John F. Kennedy, who was the first to introduce Affirmative Action and equal opportunity into the workplace, and his brother Robert F. Kennedy were both assassinated during this era. There was no way Jimi Hendrix should have become what he was during those times - times that gave America race riots in cities like Watts in Los Angeles, Cleveland, Ohio, and Chicago; times that gave us the Vietnam war in which four student protestors were shot to death by members of our own National Guard on the campus of Kent State University in Ohio. How did this happen? People accepted him for who and what he was: a black man who could play the hell out of a guitar.

Jimi was a walking, talking self-help manual. He had every reason to forgo his dream of playing the guitar, and it would have been understandable. He was born left-handed during a time when there were no left-handed guitars made. This is why he played the instrument upside down, allowing him create his unique sound. If this wasn't enough, he was self-taught, and never knew how to read sheet music. What made Jimi the legend he still is today was that Whites and blacks alike accepted him for who he was. No one demanded that he change his style, and it probably wouldn't have mattered much, anyway. By all accounts, Jimi was his own man, and wasn't persuaded to walk to the beat of someone else's drum. Being a left-handed, black guitarist playing hardcore rock made him unique. His talents made him great, but the world's acceptance of him made him Jimi Hendrix.

*Jimi Hendrix paints the picture of diversity by illustrating what people can become if they are not forced into a box to make others feel comfortable. He set an example for anyone who says: 'I can't do it because...' He didn't allow the lack of resources to keep him from playing, nor did he let his lack of formal training keep him from learning his craft. Jimi's skin color alone during the '60s was enough to keep him in bondage, forced to suppress his talents because of the stigma of skin tone. In spite of that, he didn't let fear or anger control his destiny. He took the resources he had and used his diverse skill sets to create something beautiful and powerful beyond measure: music.*

Discovering Jimi changed the way I saw potential in myself. Demographics no longer formed a line of demarcation in my abilities. Jimi was a black man just like me, but he was playing hardcore rock music. At the time, this was uncommon for our group. There were no Lenny Kravitz's or Prince's around then. Jimi was the first. He challenged the status quo and became extraordinary. This showed me that taking risks on my own abilities could work for me if I wasn't afraid to be judged by others. It was proof that diversity didn't rip one person's opportunities away and give them to another, like many detractors claimed. To the contrary, it creates more chances for success by paving new paths.

Recently, a colleague sent me a link from National Public Radio (NPR) featuring a violin duo called Black Violin. If the name of the group leads you to believe that the artists are black, then you're correct. Kev Marcus and Wil Baptist, who make up the group, hardly look like classical violinists in the traditional sense. Kev looks like he'd be tackling an NFL quarterback on Sunday afternoons. Wil B.

on the other hand looks more like a hip-hop artist then some hip-hop artists do. What makes this duo so unique is not their race or any other physical characteristic, but instead, the way they've weaved their cultural experience into the mastery of playing a classical instrument like the violin. By fusing hip-hop rhythms with a blend of unorthodox strokes, their music reminded me of Jimi Hendrix playing his rendition of the Star-Spangled Banner at Woodstock. What Kevin and Wil did was to take their life experiences and make them work together to create an opportunity for themselves. Growing up listening to hip-hop and being classically trained on an instrument uncommon for their demographic group allowed them to break the mold and develop new ways to play the violin.

It's safe to say that Kevin and Wil B probably wouldn't fit in with the New York Philharmonic or Boston Symphony Orchestra. These institutions are rich in tradition and stay true to the integrity of classical music. Very few orchestras in the U.S pay well like these two compared to the thousands of classically trained musicians who graduate each year. Therefore, a host of untapped talent will never be discovered. But this is the magic of diversity for risk takers like Kevin and Wil. Instead of limiting their options by following the status quo, they forged their own opportunity by creating an entirely new style of music; one that gives them the creative freedom that traditional orchestras don't allow. They didn't go the traditional route and stifle their talents. These men navigated their way to new horizons like Hendrix did and launched careers for themselves which otherwise wouldn't have existed. I was once told that if you don't see an opportunity, you aren't looking hard enough. Over my years as an employee, I learned that there is a sequel to this quote: "When there aren't any opportunities, create one." Diversity, in its truest form, allows for both to happen simultaneously. It encourages individuality that can lead to creative problem solving, unique ideas, and opportunities that never existed before. For those who have given up on your dreams or have psychologically quite because you didn't fit into your work environment: this one's for you.

*Over the course of my life, I've seen people become discouraged in work environments that they don't fit into. Security was often the reason they stayed, feeling the need to remain in their situation in order to support their families and pay the bills. However, there's no security in losing one's self-identity for an organization that doesn't value the whole you. Eventually you'll wake up and not remember who you are. As Steve Jobs put it, "Your time is limited, so don't waste it trying to be somebody else." Anything other than the authentic you is being someone else. If you find yourself not fitting into your organization, whether for moralistic reasons or because you're not being appreciated, maybe it's time to take your talents to a place where they'll be embraced and properly utilized. Always remember: if the name on the business isn't yours, there's no real security for you in working there. No one owes you any inheritance from it. As the CEO of "YOU Inc." you are the only security you have.*

I encourage anyone reading this book to ask yourself: "If my employer came to me right now and said "you're fired," would I be to able provide for myself or family? Would I be able to survive? If not, find out how to create opportunities for yourself by using your unique abilities and skill sets. Do what you love even if it's only as a hobby or a side gig. You may be surprised at how good you are at it. When you're ignored and feel unappreciated for your work, *Represent* yourself, *Include* your ideas, and you will *Perform* well because you love what you're doing. That's your individual diversity.

## Never Take Your Image for Granted

One of the most important attributes for anyone conducting diversity training is the image portrayed to the audience. The manner in which one presents themselves in front of people should never be taken for granted. I've learned, from sitting in audiences, that a presenter's image has much to do with gaining or losing credibility. I'm not talking about attractiveness or physical fitness - those things can help as long as everything else about the speaker's image is on point. What I'm speaking of is a presence, which commands attention and exudes expertise. It grabs you with both hands and says: "You need to hear what I'm about to say."

As a young man, I had an experience that illustrated the power of personal image. My father owned an auto body shop and my brothers and I spent our weekends and summers working there. Early one morning, we arrived at the shop and I ran inside to turn on the dusty overhead lights. Once my pupils adjusted, I froze in my tracks. In the middle of the floor sat the most gorgeous frost-blue vehicle I'd ever seen. In my short, but experienced, seven years, I'd seen many rides, but nothing like this one. It was a cross between a spaceship and a grasshopper with its four round headlights wrapped in chrome and its stretched-out front end standing out with boldness. The hood adorned a leaping cat that looked like it was in full attack mode. It was a 1974 Jaguar XJ6. I jumped inside and for a split second it felt like I'd entered someone's living room. The seats were supple like a broken-in leather sofa, and the wood grain, which wrapped around the dashboard was finished with highly polished lacquer. I thought to myself, "I'd get all the girls in this baby!"

Suddenly the shop's side door opened and jolted me out of my fantasy. I jumped out of the car, and standing before me was this tall, super cool black man. He was dressed to the nines in a dark pinstriped suit, polished black wing-tip shoes you could see your reflection in, and a blue paisley tie. His wire-framed glasses sat firmly on the bridge of his nose and reflected the sun off of his smooth, shiny baldhead. He was the epitome of cool, but without trying to be. I knew he was different, not some cat from the neighborhood trying to show off. He had a look of weathered confidence, like he'd been through some things and learned how to incorporate them into his swagger. "Hello sir, may I help you?" I asked. He looked down at me and said, "I'm here to check on my car. Is Mr. Richardson in?" "No sir, he's not, but he'll be back in a few minutes. Which car is yours?" He turned towards the Jaguar and said, "That one." A surge of energy ran through my body. With a stutter I asked, "You mean *this* Jaguar?" He nodded his glossy baldhead. For the next twenty minutes I interrogated this poor guy, asking him everything from what sort of job he had to where he'd found the car, and how fast it would go. The only thing that saved him from my barrage of questions was my father's return. I was like a Pit bull pup nipping and circling his ankles. I was so impressed by this man's image that it was etched in my brain for the rest of my life. His appearance said, "Wherever I stand, I own!" This man had no way of knowing the impression he left on me. He gave me the blueprint on how to be distinguished, with style and self-confidence. He represented all the attributes my parents demanded of my brothers and me: standing up straight, being well groomed, speaking with authority, wearing clothes and not letting them wear you! He was living proof of the values my parents instilled in us.

The experience made me realize the power of personal image and the influence it has on people; something I would need to perfect in order to deliver an effective message. A neat, well-groomed image demands attention and establishes credibility for the presenter. Together with a well-designed training program, image creates a brand that people remember. It makes individuals feel like they're part of something special. A professional appearance is part of the total presentation, and should never be taken for granted. I've never given a lecture and had someone tell me, "If you had just been a bit sloppy and disheveled, it would've increased your credibility." On the contrary, I've had participants in my classes comment in surveys how much they appreciated the professional appearance and manner in which I taught a class. In my current role as Program Manager for Senior Leadership Training for the Department of Defense, I demand that every member of my team be well-groomed and wear appropriate business attire. As subject matter experts, we have to be one step above our audience in dress and appearance. I want anyone attending our courses to know that we take our jobs seriously and put in the time to prepare for them. Look the part, act the part, be the part, and people will take notice.

What does it take to have a professional appearance? If you wear a suit, make sure it's clean and pressed. There's nothing worse than seeing egg or grease dripped on a lapel, or hanger marks on trousers. Pants bunched up around the ankles like blankets wrapped around your feet are unappealing. Hemming pant legs is cheap, quick, and easy. If that's too much of a hassle, go to a drugstore and find stitching tape. All you have to do is fold the pant legs under, stick the tape in the cuff, and use a hot iron to melt the tape. Make sure the collars on all shirts are clean and fit properly. You don't want to look like a five-year-old playing dress up in Daddy's closet. Price is irrelevant; no one knows or cares how much spent on your attire. It's about fit and appearance. Women, just follow the same rules along with your own, and you'll be just fine.

Diversity training has such a negative reputation that every aspect of presenting the material must be well orchestrated. When Harvard University writes a review describing how ineffective diversity training has been over the years, you'd better bring your A, B and C-games when it's time to teach it. Everything about your message must be on point in order to connect with the audience. All eyes will be on you, watching your every move as if waiting for the right moment to strike. Walking into a classroom can feel like entering shark-infested waters without a spear or steel cage to protect you. Don't dare mispronounce a word or have a typo on a PowerPoint slide. Miscues like these are like blood in the water for the detractor sharks waiting to destroy your credibility. Add that to an unkempt appearance and it's a recipe for disaster. I've witnessed instructors spend valuable time trying to defend themselves (or a mistake on a slide) instead of presenting their material. Mistakes like these are indefensible for any public speaking arena, but even more so when it comes to teaching diversity. I've made them on occasion when in a rush, but that's never an excuse, human error or not. Stigmas and stereotypes about the abilities of minorities set the tone for expectations before one word is ever spoken. If a participant has already decided he or she just doesn't like you or your message, they will certainly try to embarrass you. When they are truly looking out for you, they pull you aside and advise you of the mistake.

*If, as a presenter, you think all you have to do is lay out your credentials and people will listen to you for those reasons only, you are mistaken and are taking your audience for granted. Achievements and credits may get you an invitation to speak, but they won't get you repeat requests. Being memorable for positive reasons does. A presentation is more than delivering information in a systematic way for people to understand. It includes commanding respect, establishing credibility, and the ability to influence. Personal appearance is critical to achieving all three, especially for women and minorities. In most cases, women and minorities aren't afforded the same level of respect and credibility as White males, no matter what their credentials are. No one likes to admit it, but White males are viewed as the standard for all things important, including public speaking. They are the power brokers within our society. I don't see this as a disadvantage, but rather as a reminder that I have to be at the top of my game at all times.*

## **The Inner Image**

One of my college professors once told me: when you're conducting research properly, you have no idea where it will lead you. He was right. My search to understand diversity and create a professional image led me to discover how insignificant my color and race was to the concept. I found nothing that predetermined my success or failure to perform a task or make a decision, which was directly the result of my physical traits. I realized that there were imaginary boundaries placed around me that I allowed to define me. Throughout this book, I refer to 'blacks' using a lowercase 'b' for the purpose of illustrating a point. As far back as elementary school, I was taught that black in the context of race was never capitalized when written, but White as a race was always capitalized. No one ever explained why this was, but it sent a message that black people were less significant than other races. Hispanic is capitalized and it's not even a race; it's an ethnicity. Still, today, when referring to race, "black" is still sometimes written in lowercase by some of the most respected journalist and media outlets in the country. Pick up a newspaper or book and there's a good chance you may see it written that way, too. I accepted being referred to as 'black' and used it synonymously for race because I fell into the status quo. Although Jimi Hendrix destroyed the talent barriers for me, I allowed others to dictate my image and how I saw people who looked like me. Discovering diversity unlocked the mental shackles that imprisoned the negative perceptions I had of myself. To believe that all of me - mind, body, and soul, could be described by an inaccurate representation of skin color was ridiculous. No demographic trait describes or determines my talents or abilities, especially when the description is not accurate.

I'm not [b]lack! It's a made-up category to which negative connotations are attached. Pop open a dictionary and find the word 'black'. It's described by phrases such as: "Marked by tragedy, disaster, full of anger or despair." Maybe someone wants all of this to happen to me, but that's not my life and it's not the life of many brown folks I know. The label 'black' is further defined as: "people of a group with the darkest skin." Does that include people from India? I've seen some Indian brothers and sisters who are darker than most black people I know yet this description doesn't include them. Even the negative clamp on jumper cables is black. Come on, really! All the colors in the world and the black one just had to be negative? I'm brown in color, and Whites aren't white. According to every paint swatch and crayon box I've seen, they are closer to peach than white. The entire concept of race and color is senseless and serves no purpose in society, let alone the workplace. I'm a hue-man! Colored man. When I hear elderly people use the phrase "colored people," it doesn't bother me. After all, the word 'hue' means color or shade of color. Hell, it's more accurate than black. Break the word 'human' apart and you have 'colored man'. I'm good with that.

It's important for me to make this point because it's a barrier to understanding what diversity is and how it works. We as a society have adopted these inaccurate depictions of people for the purpose of maintaining inferiority. In this case it doesn't matter if all Whites are superior as long as everyone else is inferior. If I can label your skin color as something negative, evil, and illiterate, I don't have to be superior or accomplished within my own race because there's always someone deemed the true inferior people. It gives the unaccomplished and unsuccessful a buffer between themselves and true failure. Every other race then fights for what's left, vowing not to be at the bottom.

My position is not to disown my race, but to acknowledge it for what it really is. The same way I'm not dismissing diversity as a concept, but addressing what it is and what it isn't.

I can say that color has given me one thing that's critical to diversity: "life experience filled with challenges." Being labeled 'black' has given me a different experience in the world compared to people from other races. Discrimination made me navigate through life in a nonlinear way; meaning there weren't any sequential steps I could take towards success. I had to improvise. I used the military to help me pay for college and get into the State police. It was my path to becoming acceptable as a citizen. I could never take for granted that I was an American. Society would always remind me that I was still black by not acknowledging me whenever I walked into a store or having people lock their car doors whenever they saw me coming. Biologically, skin only makes up sixteen percent of the human body. I still have eighty-four percent left to offer. That eighty-four percent is responsible for my talents and capabilities. Once I realized I was allowing myself to be measured by this backwards math, I stopped using it. When it comes to people, what lies beneath the skin is what makes personal image memorable.

*To put diversity in the right context, we must put everything that deals with human relations in its proper context as well. Demographics do not dictate a person's abilities or skill sets, but they do serve to give us unique life experiences, which differ from group to group. Overt and covert oppression was my experience, but I wouldn't allow it to keep me from my goal of discovering diversity. Success was the house I wanted to enter, so no closed door leading to opportunity was going to deter me. As a law enforcement officer, I learned a valuable lesson from burglars I arrested, which helped develop my mentality: A door only closes one way, but it can be opened many ways. You can use a key, have someone else open it, pick the lock, break the glass and reach in, pull the hinges, or simply kick it in. To get into the house of success, I needed to get through the door. Shedding the extra weight of inaccurate assessments of things like color allowed me to be more agile so I could get through the door a little easier. After trying this a few times, I learned an even greater lesson: If I built my own house of success, I'd have control of all the doors. Now, the world can refer to my dark skin however it wants to. I know myself to be hue-man; a person of color born in America. By the fourteenth amendment, that makes me an American. African American.*

# 7

## PUTTING THINGS IN ORDER

### Establishing Workplace Diversity

In the introduction of the book, I said this wasn't a how-to guide on diversity. I'm going to keep my word, but there are a few things I've encountered over the years that I believe can help organizations get on the right track when implementing diversity. On a weekly basis, I receive calls from practitioners who are stressed out trying to run diversity programs for their organizations. The most common concern is that they've been given the responsibility to run these programs, but no real authority or guidance on how to make it happen. They're confused. They ask: Where do we start? What needs to be done first? These questions all come from people with advanced degrees, some of whom have doctorates, so intellect isn't the issue. Lack of clarity is the problem - clarity about how to incorporate a concept that has yet to be accurately defined.

When asked what they'd like to accomplish, the answer I most often get is: "Our organization is looking to bring in more diversity. We want 'more' women and people of color." Without knowing it, they've set themselves up for failure. To want more is not wrong, but unless there is a clear understanding of how to achieve it and why it's important to the organization, the same mistake of counting heads will be repeated over and over again. I explain to them that although Affirmative Action is an important aspect of diversity, it's not the sole answer. It only supports the first pillar, "Representation." The diversity they seek will elude them because, as stated earlier, diversity is an active process, not a state of being. It doesn't happen because people are different: it happens because our differences are actually assets used to inspire organizations to excel. That's if those assets are welcomed and included. We are all unique, and our experiences make us who we are. We are all small pieces to a bigger puzzle called life. When that's realized and celebrated, magic happens. People and companies flourish. America flourishes. That's what diversity is about.

Occasionally, I will ask my callers to lay out their plan for achieving their goals. In return, I've received well-written, thoughtful, ambitious plans for conducting Affirmative Action, which is designed to attract, seek out, promote, and train members from underrepresented groups. The plans hit every mark, including having ERGs (Employee Resource Groups), outreach teams, and recruiting drives designed to recruit women and minorities. These are great ideas for Affirmative Action, but this isn't diversity. These things help to support diversity only if and when it is attained.

These steps are missing a key ingredient, persuasion - persuasion to get people do what you want them to do. Remember diversity has a performance component to it that requires employers to be engaged with their employees on a more personal level. Affirmative Action doesn't have this requirement. We aren't talking about being friends we're talking about getting to know who employees are and what they can do. The easiest way to do this is by showing them that the organization cares about them as people first! Employers who don't make the connection between having a diverse workforce and performance often find themselves recruiting when the numbers of women and minorities are low, rejecting them when they don't fit into the organizational culture and then recruiting them again when pressured to do so. It's a practice that's been around since the institution of work was established. For decades, non-profit organizations like the military, law enforcement, and fire departments never had to recruit. Young boys grew up wanting to join these heroic organizations. Boys could easily identify with them because they were socialized to. Toy stores were filled with fire trucks, police cars, water pistols, and the famed little green army men that I still have somewhere, packed away at my parent's house. Sections within the store were divided based on sex: boys had their aisles; girls had theirs. The difference between them was that toys in the boys' aisles were based on careers. The girls' aisles were based on serving men, taking care of children, and beauty - make-up, dolls, and easy-bake ovens.

It was always a man's world, and women would probably argue it still is. White, heterosexual, Christian males were the major recruiting source, and they applied in droves! There wasn't a need for any other group to apply. Organizations didn't have to put forth any effort. They only needed to market themselves to the public and, presto, potential candidates showed up. However, what some have termed "the browning of America" (the increasing population of African-Americans and Hispanics) has forced organizations to reassess their recruiting efforts. No longer can White men be the only source of talent. Like the Industrial Age, the United States must tap into the talents of women and minorities to compete in a global world. The game has changed, and everyone is playing catch-up. You can't set up a booth in a mall anymore and catch diversity walking by. We are still talking Affirmative Action, in this case. When I explain this to the practitioners who call, their frustration doubles - one, because they've spent a lot of time putting their plans together; two, because they realize they are off course in their pursuit of diversity. They've been given an enormous undertaking that cannot be accomplished alone.

Diversity requires a cultural shift in the way organizations view their employees. Workers can no longer be singularly identified by demographic characteristics like race, color, or gender. They must be seen as valued employees. Yes, employees: this isn't a misprint. When people are categorized in the workplace by demographics, they are seen as "workers," not employees. Psychologically, they aren't considered full-fledged members: they just work for the organization. In this sort of organizational culture, these employees will never be completely accepted and they will never give their best efforts. This is where my years of experience as a commissioned officer in the military and New York State Police have been invaluable. From a position of leadership, I'm able to see the negative effects workplace culture has on an organization's morale and ability to perform at high levels. As I rose up the ladder in rank, my responsibilities broadened and my sight picture became larger. I was no longer accountable to myself: I had other people under my supervision that I was responsible for. To be an effective leader and supervisor, I had to put some of my personal beliefs, likes, dislikes, and pet peeves on the shelf. You must do some of these things, at times, to fully embrace diversity. I wasn't working for myself; it wasn't about me. I joined the organization it didn't join me. I was hired to support and carry out its interests. Therefore, it was about getting the best for the organization, by getting the best out of the employees who worked under my supervision. Notice I didn't say, "work for me."

Since I'd experienced diversity both as a minority subordinate and as a minority in a position of leadership and supervision, I saw the fault lines in what people thought created the concept. I saw the effects of misunderstanding diversity from both an employee and leadership perspective. As a consultant and advisor on the subject, this dual experience has enabled me to provide my clients with a more in-depth understanding on diversity. I'm not a theorist. I'm a practitioner. My job is to explain workplace diversity, teach it, and help others discover it so they can thrive.

## **Key Contributors**

Experience taught me that no other group in the workplace needs to understand the concept more than White men. Before anyone gets pissed off, hold your horses while I explain. It's not just because White men are accused of all the racism and discrimination that occurs: It's important for them to understand because they hold nearly all of the top leadership positions in every aspect of work - educational systems, military, science, health services, law enforcement - you name it. Their chances of leading diverse groups of people are inevitable with the rapid demographic shifts to our population. If White men fail to learn the true meaning of diversity and how to use it, all of us will suffer the consequences. With them, our power base rests. I used to hate hearing the phrase "just get over it" when people didn't want to hear others complain about racism and discrimination, but I think it's fitting here. "We all need to get over it, change has already occurred." All of us have to deal with things in life that we don't like or agree with, but great leaders lead all of their people, not just the ones they like or feel comfortable with. Great leaders are what they want their employees to be. They set the example for the entire organization. If he or she believes in diversity, the company, business, or institution will reflect it. Those employees who don't will either put on a good show and act like they do, or leave. Maybe they will adjust and just get over it!

## **Span of Control vs Span of Authority**

Many people are familiar with the term "Span of Control." There are a few variations of it, but most commonly, it refers to the number of employees a supervisor can effectively manage. It's all about numbers. When it comes to diversity, "Span of Control" represents something different. It's not about managing numbers, but the ability to 'manage' *Inclusion + Performance,* two of the three components that make up diversity. The first component, *Representation,* is not in the organization's span of control.

Contrary to popular thinking, no organization, whether it's military, law enforcement, a for-profit or nonprofit group, has the control to create diversity within the workplace the way they imagine they do. The military is an all-volunteer force, which people have to want to join. But guess what? Every organization, business, institution, or the like is voluntary. If people don't voluntarily apply for employment, the institution known as 'work' takes a hit for the respective organization. It will have to figure out how to get people to work for them. Therefore, 'the people' have the control over their *Representation,* not the organization. This is why so many businesses and organizations find themselves repeating the same efforts to recruit women and minorities year after year, decade after decade, without much success. For them, low representation of women and minorities means a lack of diversity. Because they've been led to believe that representation alone is all that's needed, their initiatives die a slow death. Eventually they become what I refer to as "walking-dead organizations." They approach diversity like zombies, aimlessly looking for minorities, qualified or not, to sink their teeth into. Rarely are these encounters productive. Like the zombies on TV, these organizations are slow and unemotional and just need a warm body to catch so they can exist another day. The living humans easily escape their misguided pursuit and find safety in the few companies and institutions that have figured out that diversity is an active process requiring full engagement from employer to employee and employee back to the organization. Once in awhile, the zombie organizations get lucky. They catch the living off guard and take a bite. Only in this real-life scenario, the living humans don't change into brain-dead corpses with insatiable appetites. They become employees - employees who aren't sincerely wanted, but needed for the purpose of saying, "Look, we have diversity!" They realize their value only serves as a 'check the box' statistic. At times these new hires come into the organization ill prepared not from the lack of intelligence, but from lack of familiarity. They're first generation employees, the way I was the first in my family to have a career in law enforcement. They don't have an Uncle Gary or an Aunt Suzy who works or worked for the organization to help prepare them for this new journey.

Finding it difficult to understand the culture of their work environment, they are prone to make mistakes; some of which aren't serious, but are enough to make them targets for those who don't believe they belong there in the first place.

Within the first year of employment (or, in the case of the military, after the first tour of duty), they're out of there. Down goes the number and away goes the misinterpreted diversity. Since *'Representation'* rests with the people, the organization can't force them to stay, just as they can't force them to apply. This is when the art of persuasion I mentioned earlier becomes critical. Being able to speak to a potential candidate who knows nothing about your company, and convince him or her that working for your organization will change their life for the better, requires persuasion. It also takes persuasion to keep an employee loyal so they won't want to leave the organization. I'm sure everyone has seen that person who loved their company so much they have to be forced to retire. They eat, sleep, and breathe the organization. When they finally leave, they keep returning to the office like Jason in the movie 'Friday the 13th'. They just can't stay away because they love the environment. Persuasion is the one tool that organizations have to create diversity within a diverse workforce. It's the device that affords them the ability to get the *Representation* needed to complete the diversity equation. Fail to persuade and you fail at diversity.

All organizations have the *authority* to do things their way. They can develop successful practices, policies and programs to create and enhance diversity however they wish. This is what I coined the "Span of Authority." The Department of Defense, along with each branch of the military has created their own diversity instructions, policies, departments and guidelines. They have the 'authority' to design and implement programs to support diversity efforts as they see fit. The same is true for companies. There are no laws, local, state, or federal, which mandate diversity as there are with Affirmative Action and Equal Employment Opportunity. That being the case, organizations can decide for themselves what's important to include in their diversity programs.

My suggestion is that organizations focus on controlling what they have the authority to do: create environments that are welcoming to *all* employees. One way to accomplish this is by taking time to ensure that new employees have sponsors who actively engage with new members their first few weeks (maybe even months) on the job. The sponsor should be there to greet the person as they walk through the front door the first day. This sends a message to the employee that they are valued and the organization is eager to bring them on board. Think about your first day on the job. Did you walk around looking for where to report? Were you told to come to an office or find your own department? This can be nerve-racking. You're probably already nervous trying to make it in on time and wanting to make a good impression on your boss. It's like going to high school on the first day of freshman year with all of those new textbooks slipping out of your hands trying to find your homeroom. Have you ever experienced walking into the wrong classroom the first day? That feeling can be the same for minorities and women walking into the organization the first day if no one's there to greet them or tell them where to go first.

Having a sponsor that takes the newbie on a field trip around the facilities helps employees learn the physical environment and become familiar with the role of other departments. Getting the 'lay of the land' is important because it can quell the anxiety of getting lost in an unfamiliar place. Any place I've ever visited, whether for a speaking engagement, visiting a client, or staying in a hotel on vacation, I felt more comfortable once I became familiar with my environment. It helped me to relax subconsciously and work more efficiently. I've worked in organizations where employees weren't given a proper orientation. Months would go by before anyone realized there was a new hire in the building. It got to a point where if I saw the person more than once, I'd walk up, introduce myself, and ask if they worked for the organization. This always made them feel better, and some would say, "You're the first person I've met outside my work space." That wasn't good, considering I was on the road at least half the year, conducting training.

It's crucial to choose the right person to be a sponsor. They're the ambassadors for the organization. If they're not a "people person," think about finding someone else. Note that outside of the interview, this is a newbie's first introduction to the company. First impressions aren't always accurate, but they do make a lasting imprint. When my youngest son was entering high school, we went to an orientation at a private school in upstate New York. Instead of having an adult faculty member escort parents and future students through the orientation, a student of the same age and grade was given the responsibility. At first I thought it was a little strange; but within the first five minutes, I understood why they took this approach. The young man who escorted us was so articulate, respectful, and engaging that I decided my son would attend the school before the tour was over. This kid not only impressed me, but impressed my fifteen-year-old as well! I found out after the tour that this young man wanted to be involved with the school's orientation program, and volunteered to give up his Saturday to do it. He believed in his institution, so he was willing to recruit other talented students to enroll there. Because of him, we were sold on the school! He represented his organization well. This is what a sponsor must do, convince the new hire that there is no better place in the world for them to work. This is also what happens when minorities and women become committed to their organizations. They become the organization's best recruiters because they are walking, talking testimonials for how the company or institution embraces a diverse workforce.

Employees who experience this sort of welcoming not only appreciate it, but are likely to be inspired to give more to the organization. If you're an employer, ask them one day. I'm willing to bet they'll echo what I've stated here, and then some. For many people, it may have been the first time anyone has ever gone to such extent to make him or her feel welcomed. In this fast-paced world, it's an advantage to take the extra time for some common courtesy and kindness. Doing so will make your company that much more successful at incorporating diversity. If your organization wants to incorporate the concept, make it easy on yourself and use the authority you have to create a culture, which welcomes everyone who walks through your door. Doing this will attract the right people from diverse groups into your organization. Word of mouth spreads quickly: the new hires will discuss their experiences with family and friends. All of them will promote the organization to others. Then you'll never have to look for numbers. Work environments that place emphasis on abilities first and embrace the whole-person concept will attract more diverse employees than they need. Put Span of Control and Span of Authority in order and there's a good chance you will get the right kind of diversity that propels your organization forward.

## Playing your Role

No matter what your title or position, you're a manager when it comes to diversity. You are responsible for making it work or causing its failure. Everyone from the CEO of a Fortune 500 company to a four-star General within the armed forces is a diversity manager. This is not a demotion it's their role in the process. Leaders at this level create the policies and guidelines that affect how people are recruited, promoted, trained, and retained. All of these functions move employees from one position to another within the organization. Where these people end up, the roles they'll play, the ideas they'll bring, is determined by those who hold leadership or supervisory positions. If you are one of these people, you are a diversity manager. You manage the *'Representation'* of minorities and women once they enter your workplace, the amount of *'Inclusiveness'* they will experience, and the level of *'Performance'* each of them will render. Most employees will comply with whatever assignment, task, or order given to them in the workplace. This is a certainty for members of the military and other paramilitary organizations like police agencies and fire departments. They have to comply or risk going to jail, being dishonorably discharged, or fired. But strong diversity managers work diligently to get employee commitment, not compliance. Commitment gives you maximum "Performance," the last link in the *"functional equation" Representation + Inclusion + Performance = Diversity.*

## **Gate Keepers**

Recruiters are diversity managers specifically responsible for the part of diversity that is *Representation*. They are the ambassadors and voice of their organizations. Whatever impression a recruiter leaves on a potential hire reflects on the company. I recall speaking with a couple of recruiters from a federal agency many years ago who shocked and disappointed me. I wanted to get accurate information concerning qualifications to join their agency. One of my professors suggested I consider this organization due to my background in law enforcement and degree in criminal justice. I was excited about the prospect, especially since the agency was looking to hire more minorities. The first recruiter I spoke with, who was male, told me I didn't qualify because the university that I received my degree from wasn't a traditional college. This was the late '90s when distance learning and online degrees weren't mainstream. I attended Empire State College in New York, which at the time was one of the non-traditional universities offering students that worked fulltime a way to earn their degrees through online and distance learning courses. Considering I'd been told 'no' before when applying for a job, I learned one thing: Never accept 'no' from someone who doesn't have the authority to say 'yes.'

After I hung up, I called my professor and told her about my experience. To describe her reaction as livid would be putting it mildly. She asked me for the recruiter's name, and when I told her, she let out a few choice words and said: "That bastard is doing it again!" She told me this was the second time he'd told someone she referred that they weren't qualified, for the same reason. She immediately contacted the agency to report the incident. In turn, the student she referred was allowed to apply and successfully made it into the organization. She told me to give her a few minutes and she'd call me back. Since I wasn't satisfied with what the recruiter told me, I decided to contact a different one to see if what the first guy told me was misinformation on his part, or a flat-out lie. I located the number for a branch in New York City. Since the Big Apple was such a metropolis of diverse people, I figured my encounter would be more welcoming.

A female recruiter greeted me. I thought this call had to go better than the previous one. Since she was a woman, I assumed she must have gone through hell, herself, to get into the agency. She would definitely understand my issue. Not so! After introducing myself, I explained what happened with the first recruiter, and that seemed to be my first mistake. She angrily asked: "Why are you calling me?" I said, "I'm calling to make sure I'm getting the right information. I don't want to miss out on an opportunity because of misinformation." Without hesitation, she said: "Let me give you some advice. If I were you, I wouldn't be calling around asking about information that one recruiter already gave you. If he were to find out, what sort of person do you think he'd feel he was dealing with?" I couldn't get the words out fast enough: "I would think this person was diligent, ambitious, and turns over every stone to find what they're looking for. You must understand, ma'am, I've been told 'no' several times in my professional careers, only to discover that it was a 'personal no' and not a 'policy no,' in each case. Had I taken the information I was given to be accurate and factual, I wouldn't be a State Trooper, or an officer in the military. I'm sorry for taking up your time. Have a nice day."

Just as I was about to call my professor back, the phone rang. It was the first recruiter. His demeanor had completely changed. He spoke to me as if I was actually a potential candidate. I didn't have to ask him anything. He gave me more information than I could've ever memorized in one phone call. My professor called me a few minutes later and asked if he had called me back. I told her yes and she asked if I received adequate information. I told her I did. She never said who she knew in the agency, but from the change of attitude, they must have been influential. I didn't tell her about the call I made to the female recruiter in NYC. For some strange reason, I was too embarrassed. Unfortunately, I was so turned off by the way I was treated I never applied for the position. I blame myself for that part. It's probably exactly what they hoped I would do. They were the gatekeepers and I allowed their reactions to deter me from entering their organization. I felt that if this was how the organization treated potential candidates, how would they treat me if I became a member? Gatekeepers know that unwelcoming treatment will deter certain people from applying, and that's why they do what they do. I allowed them to unjustifiably shut the door in my face, and this is why I blame myself for not pushing the issue.

If I decided to join that agency, the recruiters would have given their organization the first step in accomplishing diversity: *Representation*. Although I made the first contact, the opportunity to make their workplace population more diverse was theirs for the taking. Instead, it was an opportunity missed. I met all the criteria: college graduate, military veteran, State Trooper, within the age limits, and yes, African-American; not black. Most of these characteristics were never disclosed. Neither recruiter ever asked me about my skills or accomplishments. For whatever reason, they seemed more focused on deterring the type of candidate they'd advertised to be looking for. Maybe the sound of my voice was "too black," as the dictionaries describe it. Maybe I came off as being too direct. I'm not sure what it was, but whatever their reason, I was made to feel like an intruder - like I'd attempted to enter a place that was off limits to me. Everything about that experience said, "People like you need not apply."

## **The Repercussions of not Diversifying**

If mine was an isolated experience, it would've been bad enough, but unfortunately, it was and still is a common occurrence. Several studies have shown that having a black-sounding name like Jamal, Curtis, or Aretha will send a resume from the desktop to the trashcan. I must have really pissed off those recruiters. My name is Gary, for crying out loud. There aren't too many more white sounding names than that! Think I'm kidding! Watch all the commercials where the guys name is Gary. It's always a white dude and he's always in trouble or in some sort of weird predicament. I guess I shouldn't feel too bad. At least I got to speak to real people instead of wasting time sending in a resume only to have it thrown out.

Cases such as this have second, third, and fourth order effects. First, recruiters may be passing over well-qualified minority applicants with unique skill sets that can be used to create a more dynamic organization. In my case, that's exactly what happened. I was a perfect applicant. My experience as a police officer and member of the military gave me special skills like firearms expertise, formal leadership training, which most organizations don't conduct, and effective report writing; all of which are requirements for the respective agency I applied to. The term 'applicant' is most important, considering that it fits the legal use of Affirmative Action. Organizations can legally set quotas to increase their pool of qualified candidates from underrepresented groups. I was only trying to apply. There was no guarantee I'd be hired, and I understood that clearly. It was up to the agency to *persuade* me to be a part of their team; something they didn't have to put much effort into, considering I'd called them. Second, the lack of foresight puts companies and businesses behind the curve when it comes to keeping pace with the needs of an evolving American society. According to the census bureau, by the year 2050, minorities will make up the majority of the U.S. population. This means that leaders will have to learn how to lead and work with diverse groups of people like never before. Without being familiar with these groups, it will be difficult to manage diversity and remain competitive in the global market. It won't be difficult to compete due to a lack of race or color, but because of the lack of cultural experience within the organization. Cultural experience in this context isn't celebrating Women's History Month or holding a bake sale with ethnic treats to feast on. What I'm talking about is critical data collection that can reveal what certain groups of customers and employees want and need from an organization or business. This is also a reason law enforcement agencies find it difficult to protect and serve citizens from various demographic backgrounds, which the particular agency I spoke of was responsible for doing. As a former police officer, experience taught me that if you can't relate to people, it's impossible to serve and protect them with the dignity and respect that all law enforcement agencies take an oath to do. Every qualified minority candidate cast aside creates a wider distance in filling the need for gaining the cultural I.Q. needed to comprehend diversity. Again, the point is not necessarily about being diverse; it's about understanding diverse opinions, ideas, and beliefs. This gets you closer to diversity.

Third, once organizations realize they need diversity in the workforce, they will have to play catch up. They start by instilling aggressive minority recruiting drives in an effort to connect with a population that's become more diverse and technologically savvy. For many businesses, it's already too late. Their brands have become irrelevant. The younger tech-savvy customers, many who are of color, know nothing about them. Their products are no longer fashionable, and their services are antiquated and no longer needed. Look at what's happening to shopping malls and many of the retail stores around the country. They're going out of business on a monthly basis. Direct shipping through the Internet caught them sleeping because they failed to understand how and why the new consumer does their shopping. If you're wondering how this relates to diversity, take a look at the economic progress and spending habits of African-Americans. Over the past decade, income growth for African-Americans has outpaced Whites in every annual household income level above $60,000, with the biggest increase evident in households making over $200,000 per annum - an increase of 138% compared to the rest of the population, which increased at 74%. Between 2013 and 2014, college enrollment for African-American high school graduates rose from 59.3% to 70.9%, exceeding that of Whites and the total population. The average age of the African-American population is also younger than other groups - it's 31.4 years of age compared to Asians at 33.8, Non-Hispanic Whites at 39.0, and the total population, at 37.7.[ii] What's also important to note is that African-Americans are, as the Neilson Report suggests, "Heavy consumers of all media types and digitally-empowered communicators."

I can personally attest to the fact that this isn't an overstatement. My father, who's in his seventies, stays glued to the Internet. He's schooled me on a few things he's come across while online, like property and rare vehicles for sale. I have purchased two cars, several items of clothing, watches, household goods, artwork, and earned my Master's degree all thanks to the internet and social media; reason being: I have a better experience. I don't have to be followed through the store as if I'm going to steal something, and don't have to hear "that one is really expensive," which is a total disregard for my personal financial status and spending power. Nope. I can sit right on my coach and treat myself with the greatest amount of respect and courtesy anyone could ever give me.

These stats may not mean much too some people, but if you're interested in how diversity works, they should. They reflect a change in economic mobility and education levels of people who, in the past, weren't considered relevant to business. If you're thinking that I'm citing these statistics as a way to show America that former slaves have overcome, you're completely missing the point. I'm revealing information that most people, including those of color, pay little attention to. This information signals change, a broadening of life experience that can be used to benefit a workplace, if used properly.

Here's something else to consider. When I'm out for a drive, my subconscious mind guides me to places I see being patronized by other people of color. I say 'subconscious' because I'm not intentionally looking for people of color so I can shop; but when I see them, I want to go inside and take a look. This has nothing to do with racism and everything to do with feeling comfortable in the environment. Most of the businesses I patronize have White proprietors - that's not a concern. As long as the business has what I want and I'm treated like a valued customer, it's fine with me. But when I see people who look like me shopping in certain stores, I get a sense that the owner is comfortable with people of color in their establishment. The same goes for dining out. Seeing those who look like me gives me a sense of security. They've co-signed the business for me, done the vetting so to speak. I feel it's a place that wants my hard-earned money. This is what I was referring to by spending habits.

As it pertains to diversity and how it works, knowing the habits and ways people operate within society are consequential to getting employees to perform the way employers need them to. It allows for interaction with individuals from their perspective and relies less on preconceived notions and unconscious biases. This is quite different from stereotyping. Not everyone within a particular race or ethnic group will respond the same way in like situations. I'm not suggesting that one size fits all. What I'm providing is a little insight on some perceptions and practices developed due to the way race and color are perceived in America.

Last, when qualified minority applicants with diverse backgrounds are passed up, the organization that passes on them loses out on a chance to connect with that community. This is an error in business. In many cases, these same applicants are also customers of the company's products and services; people who could easily give feedback on the strengths and weaknesses of the brand. It's nothing personal - it's about business and how groups of people experience things from different perspectives. Wise leaders understand they don't have to like or agree with another person or a group's perspective in order to be successful. They come to realize that to be aware is to be informed. Being aware of the different perspectives and experiences people bring to the table can help leaders manage their talent better because they can relate to employees and understand their needs. The good old days of manufacturing jobs driving the economy are gone for now. To uphold the advanced society we've created requires us to sell products and services beyond the shores of America. It's the only way to compete in a global market unless or until something changes that makes an industry more profitable. We must not forget that other countries have great talent too, which makes outsourcing attractive since most countries don't pay anywhere near the wages paid in the United States. Unless the laws change to close some of the loopholes, companies are going to outsource their goods to make more profits. From a business standpoint, it makes sense. Finding talent abroad is hard for me to digest, considering that the United States has a surplus of talent, which it doesn't use. In the meantime, what we can do to find homegrown talent is cultivate it by giving more people the opportunity to share their skills and abilities for the benefit of themselves and the country we live in. The task of keeping America great is too large for one group to manage. It's a joint venture and everyone has to pitch in. No one should complain about our welfare system if we're going to exclude people from the opportunity to work. How else will they survive?

*In order to show the value of diversity, it's important to discuss things that are least important to the concept. This is why I've mentioned color, race, and gender throughout the book. These three demographic categories are at the center of misguided principles and standards when it comes to understanding the subject. It's important to note that people need supervision, while processes need to be managed. Diversity is a process requiring management to be successful. Reliance on physical traits without consideration for the whole person - i.e. decision-making ability, emotional maturity, confidence etc. - will result in placing people in positions that may not fit their skill sets. The dots between abilities, life experience, and talent don't automatically connect with personal characteristics, no matter what their demographic makeup may be. Remember, diversity is an active process, which requires engagement from the employer to the employee; not just a collection of different people who may think differently. The latter is not enough. Thinking differently means nothing, if those having different thoughts aren't acknowledged and utilized. Progress in education and economic status of African-Americans and other minority groups has given America - not black-America, but all of America - more talent than it's ever had before. Want to make America great again! Use the talent we have, and it will be.*

# 8

## THE RECIPE

### The Organizational Approach

One of the most common questions I'm asked is: "What does it take to incorporate diversity in the workplace?" After studying the subject for seventeen years, I've learned there are certain things an organization must do in order to accomplish the brand of diversity I'm speaking of. This next section is a list of measures I feel are must-do's to gain diversity comprehension and successfully implement it into the workplace. They are not sequential steps in the process of diversity, but rather, a list of things that, in my experience, helps to create a solid understanding of the process and how it works.

**1. Consult a reputable diversity expert with a proven track record** - Think of a 'proven track record' like this: If a sprinter runs fifty races over the course of a season, but comes in last place every time, he or she has a proven track record. It's just not a good one! They went to the races, competed, but didn't do well. You need a winner: someone who's achieved positive results that can be verified. It's dangerous to rely solely on information contained on a person's website. Recommendations or testimonials can be written by the consultant who owns the site or by friends and family. If you're going to spend money on a consultant, ask him or her for names and numbers of previous clients who've used their services. If they provide them, you're off to a good start.

What you should be asking is whether the services provided by the consultant were useful in moving the organization towards the inclusion needed to attain high productivity from a diverse group of employees. Ask if the training provided is still relevant a year or two later. This is important because the foundation of workplace diversity never changes. *Representation + Inclusion + Performance = Diversity* is the foundation, which will always remain constant. The only thing that will change is the made-up categories and catch phrases used to describe it. First there was Affirmative Action; then diversity; and now its diversity and inclusion (or D&I, as it's commonly referred to). Give it time and it will be called something else. Don't become mesmerized by fancy terms and dynamic phrases like these. They are pixie dust sprinkled on paper without glue to hold them in place. As soon as the winds of challenge blow, they will disappear, and you'll have spent your money for a nice presentation and nothing else. You should ask, specifically: what did the consultant do to help the organization gain clarity on diversity and is the work applicable to our workplace environment? If they can't tell you, ask if they attended the class, used the materials, or actually saw the suggestions he or she made. If they are privy to this information, but can't answer these questions, chances are the consultant may've been a good speaker, but not a good diversity trainer.

In fairness to consultants, most of them are rarely hired under the right circumstances. Most organizations wait until they're hit with a lawsuit or have a plethora of equal employment opportunity complaints before they'll reach out for help. This puts the consultant in a tough spot. They come into an organization when it's red-hot with anger from all sides. Everyone is forced to attend the training and now they're really angry. The alleged offender is angry because someone filed a complaint against him or her, the complainant is furious because the offender wasn't fired, and those not involved in any of it are upset because they feel punished for someone else's wrongdoing. In most cases, this is a recipe for disaster. The topic of diversity is already sensitive enough due to all the misperceptions, and now people are forced to sit and listen to some stranger talk about how to "just get along." The consultant has to play counselor and therapist instead of illustrating how effective diversity can be for the organization.

Time is another disadvantage for consultants. Since most organizations don't clearly understand the difference between being diverse and having diversity, they hire the consultant to come in and pitch a class for a couple of hours, hoping it'll help employees get along better in the workplace. To expect someone to come in for such a short period of time and effect change is unrealistic. Sufficient time is needed to explain the concept and illustrate how the organization can achieve it. If a thorough needs assessment isn't conducted prior to the training, forget about it. Every business, company, and institution has different issues unique to their organization. Each concern or issue must be carefully analyzed to show how diversity should be utilized in those situations.

For instance, some organizations have meetings which department heads are required to attend, to discuss current or future projects. This is a great opportunity to implement diversity by allowing subordinates to attend some of those meetings; if for no other reason than to become familiar with the inner workings of the organization. It gives the attendee face-time with executives and senior leaders, which is vital to progressing up the ranks or corporate ladder. It's what my superiors did for me. As explained earlier, attending meetings helped me successfully navigate my way through my careers. There may also be opportunities to appoint team leads for certain projects. This is another chance to use diversity by selecting employees from diverse groups to lead or be on the teams. Steps like this can help build self-confidence and illustrate any special skill sets individuals may have. Selecting individuals with diverse backgrounds in this case isn't about putting demographics first; it's about creating opportunities for the company or institution to identify talent and utilize it for their benefit.

As a consultant, knowing how the organization operates will show where there are opportunities to create and enhance diversity. Without this knowledge, helping the client correct deficiencies is swinging at a piñata blindfolded. Each course must be specifically tailored to meet the needs of the organization, but again: the explanation of diversity must remain constant. Once the foundation of diversity is presented, only then should the consultant begin to show how to effectively implement it in the workplace.

If hired prior to negative fallouts and given the proper amount of time, a good consultant can help to positively effect change. Depending on the size of the workforce, this may take a few days or even a few weeks. Workplace culture is easy to create, but difficult to change. The consultant has to be given a realistic chance to do their job, which is providing subject matter expertise.

**2. Leadership Commitment** - Leaders don't have to be first in line on the diversity train, but they'd better be on it. Working with and for leaders over the years, I've come to one conclusion: The success or failure of diversity is the difference between having a good leader or a great one. I don't base the differences between good and great leaders on salary, title within the organization, rank, or accolades. It's based on how effective the leader is at getting people to perform at their best, regardless of who's on their team.

Great leaders have a broader vision of what's needed in the workplace because they understand it takes teamwork to have a successful organization. For the great ones, employee performance is everything. They have a vested interest in how employees perform because everything from the quality of services to the products rolling out of the door represents their leadership abilities. CEOs have shareholders and boards to satisfy, while government and military leaders have Congress and the President to answer to on how well their organizations perform. Leaders at the top of their game understand they can't afford to have sub par performance from themselves or the people who work for them. The entire organization is expected to be starting-lineup material, first-teamers, not substitutes. Ask a great leader how to get maximum performance out of their employees and I guarantee that you will consistently hear them speak about the environment within the workplace. They'll tell you that an environment, which encourages inclusion of all its employees, creates opportunities to get the best out of people.

Another characteristic separating great leaders from the good ones is that the former does something good leaders are reluctant to do: move out of the way and allow the experts to use their expertise. Why? Great leaders understand that they aren't experts on everything; and neither do they have to be. They're wise enough to get the best people to work for them, which is why they don't have to be the smartest person in the room. These leaders get smart people to perform, and performance is the final piece of the diversity equation.

A leader doesn't have to understand diversity to be great. If that were the case, there might not be many great ones out there. What they need is a clear understanding of the advantages diversity can give their organization over their competitors. This is why I placed finding a consultant with a proven record first. If consultants are knowledgeable on the concept, they'll be able to give leadership a clear understanding of diversity and how to implement it within their organizations. The great leader will then be able to leverage the talents of their employees.

**3. How to Measure Diversity Efforts** - I often ask diversity practitioners why diversity needs to be measured. Measuring diversity is a big deal for practitioners. Go to any of the job search websites and you'll find that nearly all the jobs under the category of "Director of Diversity" require performing some sort of measurement or analytics on diversity. I'm not questioning the legitimacy of this, but I'm not a fan of the manner in which I've seen it performed. Most of the measuring is based on statistics. Counting the number of women and minorities employed by the organization and the positions they're in. The reports generated from this data aren't reporting on diversity. They're reports on Affirmative Action. I've completed several of them in my roles as an Equal Employment Compliance Officer, and they aren't designed to illustrate an active process like diversity. This is *'quantitative'* diversity. Important for gauging workplace composition, employee participation in certain aspects of the organization like training, or the number and type of complaints filed during the year. However, what's needed to identify whether diversity is operating effectively is a *'qualitative'* approach.

If you want a report on diversity as it applies to work and productivity, you don't measure it: you assess it using two things - employee performance and the climate of the workplace. Since diversity is an active process, its effectiveness must be assessed and not counted. Assessing diversity from an employee perspective begins with performance and ends with productivity. Employees are hired with the hope that they'll do both at a high level, and employers want to know whether they are or not. For this reason, many organizations rely on an assessment tool like evaluations. Most evaluations I've seen over the years ask many of the right questions concerning leadership ability, decision-making skills, professionalism, and special skills the employee possesses. What most evaluations don't ask is how well the employee works with people of different cultures, ages, beliefs, sexual orientation, etc. A question like this is important, considering that evaluations are used for promotions and pay increases.

Some people may feel this is going too far with an evaluation, but I would argue that, for promotions and leadership positions, an organization should want to discover these things up front. Not knowing could put the company or institution in jeopardy when the person has to lead a diverse group of people. Most importantly, evaluations illustrate employee performance and the level of engagement they have within their organizations. When analyzed correctly, evaluations can reveal inclusiveness. Questions such as "Does the employee use any specialized skills to perform their tasks, or does the employee volunteer to take special assignments or projects?" would give some insight. If the employee answers no, it shouldn't be counted against them, since there may be circumstances, which preclude them from doing these things. But if or when they have done them, the employee should be acknowledged for it, and the company should include it as part of their diversity assessment. As for how this would be documented in a report, the more people who answer 'yes' to questions like these, the higher the score in the area of inclusion would be.

Since productivity is ultimately the reason employees are hired, I would go a step further and survey customers and end users of the organization's products and services. What I'm about to tell you will illustrate the importance of conducting something most people hate to do, which is take surveys. It's not my favorite thing to do, either. Through the years, that has changed, and here's why. Before the TV show "Undercover Boss" premiered, I used to say: "If I ran a big company I would show up unannounced, without introducing myself to the employees. This way I could get an accurate gauge on how they were performing." I'd want to know if they were motivated to work and treated customers with utmost respect and professionalism. I realize I missed out on being a famous producer by not creating the show myself; so instead, I would settle for conducting good old-fashion surveys. Climate surveys, which ask about workplace environment and customer satisfaction, are necessary. As a customer, I've experienced lousy service on a few occasions and left the business saying, "I will never go back."

I've also received some extraordinary ('extra' being the key) service, which made me a customer for life. My wife and I were out on a Sunday drive and happened to see a beautiful car sitting on the lot of a privately owned dealership. It was a small, locally owned business, so I was somewhat skeptical about the service I'd receive. I've purchased plenty of cars over the years and had my share of bad experiences with dealerships trying to jack up prices or sell me a piece of junk. Not wanting to hold every dealership liable for those experiences, I decided to call them on Monday. The next day, I called the lot and was greeted by a young lady who had a polite but enthusiastic voice. I told her I was interested in a car on their lot and had some questions about it. She said, "Okay, great! Let me get my father on the phone; he owns the business." The gentleman got on the phone and greeted me by saying: "Hello, Mr. Richardson. How may I help you today?" He didn't just say hello. He addressed me in a way that made me feel respected not just as a customer, but as a man. It made me feel important.

I asked about the price of the car and he told me, but also stated that it was negotiable, and not to worry about it. If I liked it, he would work with me. To be honest, I really wasn't in the market for a car because I already had a couple that I loved, but this car was beautiful and really sparked my interest. The owner ended the call by saying, "Come on down and take the car out for the day." I thought it was an overly-stated gesture of kindness to get me to come in. I told him I'd stop in over the weekend. My wife and I showed up on Saturday and the car had been washed and was parked out front, waiting for us. The owner's daughter met us outside and said she had the key for us. She told me her father said to take the car out for spin and they'd see us later when we returned. I waited a few minutes for her or someone else to come on the drive with us, but it never happened.

    I asked the young lady if anyone was coming with us. "Oh, no sir, my dad wants you to enjoy your day. We close at six, so just make it back by then." Huh? I looked at my watch, and it was only one o'clock. I didn't know how to take this - was it some kind of trick? If I stayed too long, would they think I was stealing the car? This was foreign to me. Once I sunk into the plush leather seats and the car automatically adjusted its shocks to the contour of the road, I forgot all about the time. I even forgot I wasn't serious about buying another car. Fifteen minutes later, my wife and I returned to the lot. I'd made up my mind. I was buying the car.

    Before we could get out, the owner met us and opened the car door for my wife. He escorted us inside and asked us to be seated. He didn't ask us anything about the car for about twenty minutes. Instead, he offered us the smoothest espresso I'd ever had. We talked, just talked. We conversed about quality of life sorts of things and who we were as human beings. I'd forgotten what I came there for until his daughter asked my wife if she liked the car. Finally, we got down to business. I told him we wanted the car and he acted as if it was already ours. He said, "That's good; my daughter will put the paperwork together for you to sign. Would you like to share a celebratory drink of Cognac?" I didn't have time to answer before he pulled out this beautiful crystal bottle that looked like something a king or queen would drink from. Not being a drinker, I had to say no three times - however, my wife read the label and said, "Hell yes, I'll try some." All I know is that it was old and from Russia.

I am now a customer for life; not because of the espresso or Cognac, but because of the way I was treated and the way they performed as an organization. If you were the CEO of this company, wouldn't you want my feedback? Wouldn't you want to know how your employees made me a lifelong customer? Maybe you wouldn't want them to offer their customers Cognac, but it helped to make me a lifelong customer. The only way to find out what's working is by surveying the customer and, more importantly, the employees who serve them. The employees will tell you what they're doing to be successful, how they're doing it, and what allows them to make it happen. If the organizational climate is harmonious you will get positive feedback from most employees; not just certain groups. It doesn't mean that everyone will be happy. You can't satisfy everyone, no matter how good the environment may be. However, you certainly don't want entire groups being unhappy, or there's a problem; even if that group is small. Assess your organizational climate and you will be on your way to assessing workplace diversity.

**4. Get the Right Tool for the Job -** If you work in corporate America or own a business, this section may not seem relevant to you; but when it comes to reporting on diversity, the climate survey is the way to do it. If this surprises you, don't worry: the military will be just as surprised when they hear this, too. They haven't discovered it yet, but if used properly, the military has the right tool for reporting on diversity. It's called The Defense Equal Opportunity Climate Survey. This survey is not specifically designed to assess diversity; nor does the military utilize it for that one purpose. However, it does contain questions that specifically deal with the R+I+P=Diversity model and here's how.

The climate assessment survey was created for commanders as means to gauge their work environments. It assists them with identifying strengths and weaknesses within their area of control and responsibility. It's broken down by individual demographics such as race, gender, ethnicity and rank. Being designed this way, it allows a leader to get a picture of the perceptions different groups have of the work environment. For this reason, demographic categories within the survey make sense. Because society has placed so much emphasis on physical characteristics, it's important to capture how different groups are treated in the workplace.

If you're wondering whether or not the leader gets open and honest responses to the survey questions, the answer is yes. Sometimes the responses are eye-openers. I've seen plenty of grown-ups shed a tear or two after reading how people truly felt about their leadership ability. People are brutally honest and leaders get to read every comment without manipulation or deletions. The surveys are anonymous and voluntary, so people let loose and share the truth - or at least what they view as being the truth.

Participants who volunteer to take the survey are asked approximately fifty questions, divided into four sections: organizational effectiveness, equal opportunity and fair treatment, sexual assault prevention, discrimination and sexual harassment. Discrimination and sexual harassment are categorized together because sexual harassment is a form of sex discrimination. Nearly all of the questions are subjective in nature; meaning, they ask how people perceive or feel concerning workplace issues. A big difference between this type of survey and metric reports is the survey gathers real-time data. It asks employees how they feel about issues "right now."

I know some people may be thinking: "How could this method of data collection be effective when everyone has an opinion?" I'm with you. It's very subjective. If someone has an axe to grind with their boss, they will express it, and the boss gets to read it. As a former Equal Opportunity Director in the military, I was responsible for administering these surveys, and they were accurate for the purpose of assessing workplace climates. Before you disagree, keep in mind that surveys are designed to capture both positive and negative opinions. Whether opinions are right or wrong shouldn't be the focus. Whether they're relevant or not should be. Leaders, business owners, and CEOs need both opinions for their organizations to evolve and meet the needs of customers and those who serve them. It's necessary to hear all opinions. You don't have to like them, but you must hear them in order to address them accordingly.

No matter what the percentage of participation - twenty percent or one hundred - there's important information to be gathered about the organization concerning diversity. Little participation may mean employees feel the survey is a waste of time and nothing positive will come of it, or they believe they'll be retaliated against for speaking their minds. In either case, the level of participation speaks to organizational climate. Enthusiastic participation could be positive or negative, as well. One organization I surveyed had a ninety-three percent participation rate. The climate in the workplace was so bad that every member spoke up! The other seven percent wrote letters expressing their anger and dissatisfaction.

The key to using these surveys to assess diversity is to have a well-versed diversity advocate analyze the data and provide management or leadership with a comprehensive report showing the climate status and issues to be addressed. The diversity advocate or expert should also point out the strengths of the organization, within the report. This will help to solidify practices that have worked well and set a standard. The reports shouldn't be used as a disciplinary tool. Participants mustn't be punished for taking it or not taking it - to do so would create a chilling effect and discourage people from taking the survey again. As long as there aren't any threats of violence or violations of any policies, there shouldn't be retribution. The surveys should be used to correct deficiencies to help organizations perform better. Honest opinions should be appreciated and taken into account.

How does this all relate to diversity? If I asked for a report on how effective your diversity efforts were as they pertain to *Representation + Inclusion + Performance = Diversity,* the issues addressed in the climate survey is exactly what I'd be hoping you could answer. The survey asks participants if they feel valued, if they feel they can perform at a high level in their environment, does discrimination occur, or if they receive valuable workplace information. All of these are indicators of inclusion or exclusion. I wouldn't care how many people from under-represented groups you were able to show on paper unless you could also tell me why those groups want to work for your organization. The composition of the employee workforce would be in your Affirmative Action Plan. I would want to know how employees or members were being included in the workplace, if they were being used to their fullest potential, how they were being treated, and how they were "performing" as an outcome of this treatment.

Knowing these human relations issues will tell me whether or not your organization has a grasp on diversity. I would know why it can't attract and keep a diverse workforce. It may also illustrate why your company is lagging behind in its sector. Maybe there aren't enough creative thinkers who are able to utilize their unique talents and experiences, or maybe the creative thinkers aren't being included. As a reminder: people do have to work, but they don't have to work for *you*. If compliance from employees is all you're after, good luck. Your competitors may be figuring out how to get commitment from theirs.

**5. Connect Discipline, Diversity and Performance -** When it comes to gaining or losing commitment, the manner in which an organization administers discipline is at the center of it. Too harsh, and it can break the will of people to be creative; too lenient, and it lowers standards for excellence. Discipline is one of the most important parts in establishing a healthy environment for diversity. When it's done correctly, it fosters teamwork and solidifies the organization's standard for high performance. During some of my training sessions, I've had White males express their reservations about administering disciplinary actions against women and minorities. They claimed they were afraid of having a discrimination or sexual harassment complaint filed against them.

This excuse for a leader not performing their duties is detrimental to the organization and to diversity. Not taking corrective action, which is the purpose for discipline, weakens the organization at its core. People will ask: "Why have rules and policies when they aren't adhered to?" It's worse if some get the book thrown at them while others get special treatment. It's also true in the reverse. When those who are deemed different are punished more harshly than others, it sends a message that they aren't valued in the workplace. Leaders at all levels of management and supervision must understand that anyone can file a complaint against them, regardless of the reason. I've had complaints of discrimination filed against me before, but never allowed them to stop me from performing my duties as a leader. I knew the policies and regulations of my organization and followed them. I kept documentation on the steps I took to correct the unacceptable behavior and showed progressive disciplinary action. Color, race, or gender didn't matter. It shouldn't matter.

Discipline must be administered, but in an appropriate manner which corrects the unacceptable behavior and clearly defines expectations for future performance. Worrying about having complaints filed against you is not a good reason to neglect your responsibilities. If you're treating people according to their performance and following the policies and guidelines of your organization, you're fine. When discipline is fair but too heavy-handed, it can shut down performance. Good employees will bounce back when treated fairly; they know when they're not performing well. If appropriate measures are used and the employee shuts down and never returns to high productivity, find another employee. In business, you can't afford to have people work for you who are too sensitive to manage the pain of constructive criticism. Although no one likes to be chastised, it's a sign of mental strength and emotional maturity to be able to handle it. Before an employee is let go, the organization should ask themselves: "Have we done enough to get the best out of them, or did we only want them to comply?"

    Coming from a diversity practitioner, this may sound harsh, but diversity doesn't require you to like everyone. Organizations must understand that the number one goal of diversity is getting optimal performance from employees; not making friends. I discovered early in my career as a Station Commander with the State Police that I didn't have to like all of my subordinates to get them to perform at their best. At times, brutal honesty about their performance and how it would reflect on their evaluations worked better than trying to be friends. I also needed their honesty on how I was serving them as their leader. Don't be shocked by the word *serving*. If you're a leader, you're serving the organization by serving the subordinates that work under your authority. Unless your name is on the bottom of their paychecks, they don't work for you - they work for the company, and so do you.

    I've told subordinates when they weren't performing at a high level and, yes, sometimes I was angry when I told them. However, I never belittled them and always had proof to back up my criticism. I knew they could perform better because they were good enough to be troopers. If they made it through the academy, then they were capable human beings. My job as a leader was to get optimal performance out of them. I can't say I had one hundred percent success every time, but each year, my station, as a whole, consistently increased its performance. From the time I arrived as the Station Commander, the amount of traffic tickets written rose by nearly ten thousand each year. Even though police agencies are not-for-profit organizations, don't be fooled. The average speeding ticket with surcharges is always over one hundred dollars. Increase the ticket count by ten thousand a year. We made money for someone.

Great companies push the envelope further to find strengths and weaknesses by conducting exit interviews. If your company, business, or institution doesn't do them, you're not getting the full picture of your work environment. Opportunities for improvement are missed and employee commitment is difficult to attain. Within the R.I.P *(Representation + Inclusion + Performance)*, inclusion means to be actively engaged at every level of the organization, and discipline is part of it. It's not doing things the black way, the LGBT way, the Hispanic way, or the White way; it's doing them the *right* way. The right way is fostering a work environment where everyone knows the rules, is given opportunities to excel, and is rewarded according to their individual performance. These are the steps to gain commitment from employees. Are you taking them?

Appropriate treatment of employees increases the opportunities for high productivity in that it's tailored according to the individual and what he or she brings to the table. When it comes to performance, appropriate treatment - not fair treatment - is the proper term. As a business owner myself, I have a wide range of options when it comes to dealing with anyone who works for me. If I assign an employee a task and it's not done to my standards, I could impose discipline by yelling at them, demoting them, taking away extra responsibilities, or simply firing them. All of these things are fair. I'm the boss. As long as I don't discriminate against them or cheat them out of their wages, I have the right to take any of the actions mentioned.

The question is, would it be appropriate? It comes down to my end game and what I want to accomplish. If I want to punish them, then those steps would be fine; but if I want them to learn from their mistakes and not be afraid to make decisions when necessary, those actions may not be appropriate. Neither would it be appropriate to give them special treatment in these cases because of their race or gender. Special treatment is a reward for special performance. Most women and minorities I know don't want special treatment, either. They just want to be treated like everyone else, even when it comes to discipline.

*For the process of diversity to take place, a clear understanding of the concept must prevail. Without knowing that Representation isn't an automatic default for skills and abilities, organizations will continue to miss the importance of experiences. It's common now to have an African-American female, who attends an Ivy League school, think and act the same as a White female who attended Yale or Harvard. If either one of these women were hired, the only difference the organization may get between them is skin color. As an active process, diversity is more sophisticated than physical appearance. Life experiences must also be considered to explore the full range of employee potential. Subject matter experts on diversity can play an important role in helping organizations establish harmonious work environments when he or she understands that the final part of the concept is performance. Leadership buy-in for diversity is vital to its success in the workplace. Since leaders are responsible for setting and upholding the standards of their organizations, what they consider important, workers will view as important. The culture within the workplace will begin to reflect the acceptance of differences required to facilitate diversity. Discipline is related to performance, as it is a corrective measure taken to uphold expectable standards set by the organization. For members of an organization to feel valued, discipline must be appropriate, timely, and designed to elevate performance. It's as much an art as it is a science in that corrective action must be situational with consideration of circumstances. How disciplinary actions are administered must be balanced and appropriate for whatever end-state the organization wants to achieve.*

# 9

# HOW DIVERSITY SHAPED MY CAREERS

## My Role as a Consultant

During my travels, I'm often asked what profession I'm in. I'm not sure why, but it's a kick-starter to escape the boredom during long flights. One hundred percent of the time, my answers lead to more questions no matter how detailed the explanation. I used to answer, "I'm a diversity consultant," expecting my curious co-passengers to know what I was talking about. The looks on their faces signaled they had no clue of what that entailed. I became more creative. "I'm a consultant on diversity," figuring if I lead with "consultant," they'd at least understand that. Not really: the diversity part was the sticking point, and made for an awkward introduction. I'd sit there in my cramped seat, smiling at my neighbor as if I was a prominent neurosurgeon whom they should've heard of. They'd stare back at me like I was a guy with a profession no one has ever heard of.

What I've realized is that I have a unique career. I assist organizations with gaining commitment from their employees in order to implement diversity into their organizations. It's unique in that 'people' are often the last asset organizations perform maintenance on. Yes: humans need maintenance, too. We are not machines or equipment, but we control them. Who makes sure that we are functioning properly? Before we break down, is there a way to ensure that we're receiving recurring maintenance so it doesn't happen? This is part of what I do as a consultant and diversity practitioner. I diagnose the issues organizations have with understanding diversity and how to implement it. People are the engine for organizational performance.

My discussion on climate surveys was to illustrate one of the tools used to diagnose the issues affecting that performance. What I prescribe is a way to gain commitment from employees by discovering barriers they face working in diverse organizations and how to overcome them. I don't demand that people change who they are or how they feel - that's up to them. I show them how to perform in spite of those things in order to give their best efforts to the organizations they work for.

This is not strictly directed towards women and minorities. A company is only as good as its worst employee, regardless of who they are and what they look like. This is especially true for the service sector. Think of a bad experience you've had at a hotel, restaurant, hospital, or department store. How did you feel afterwards? Did you tell yourself you'd never patronize their business again? If so, that hurt the entire organization's bottom line. A loyal customer maintains steady cash flow, which helps support payroll and other expenses incurred. It usually doesn't matter whether or not the CEO of that company was a genius who donates millions of dollars to charities each year. You were finished with them! Why? Performance! It was sub par and as a result, you suffered for it.

I'm the guy who tries to keep this from happening by illustrating how diversity works to enhance performance. If you're a business owner, CEO, or leader of an organization, you need optimal performance out of employees to make your business thrive. They are the backbone of your company. Employees are EVERYTHING. They can make or break your business, and it starts with a leader who recognizes that and does everything he or she can to make those employees feel valued. True diversity is about performance; optimal performance that can only come from commitment from both employee to employer and employer to employee. My job is to illustrate how to attain that commitment by assisting organizations with creating the right workplace climate. It requires a deliberate focus on creating an environment where employees feel wanted - part of a company, which recognizes, values, and rewards their contributions. Rewarding someone doesn't have to be a grand spectacle. An email or short letter of appreciation can go a long way towards motivating employees.

## Commitment to Work

Being a diversity practitioner isn't a sexy career like being a physician or an attorney. I'm pretty sure parents aren't pushing their children to attend an Ivy League college to one day become a famous diversity expert. But this is the beauty of America. In this country, you have the ability to create your own path if you are willing to keep grinding. For seventeen years, I've been able to wake up every day and live my life's passion regardless of what others know or think about it. It fulfills me like nothing else I've ever done. When I stand before a class, teaching people about the concept of diversity, I realize that in some cases, I'm helping to fulfill dreams. Not everyone wants to be rich and famous. Some people just want to go to work and be able to provide for themselves and their families. Coming home with a smile on their face because they feel appreciated by their employer is their dream.

Providing a deep understanding about a widely misunderstood concept like diversity makes me feel connected to humanity. Being able to watch a business thrive as a result of my services gives me great pride and humbles me to the idea that I'm fortunate enough to live my life contributing to society. I get the opportunity to leave the world with something.

Had I not committed myself to doing what I love and listen to my subconscious mind, I may have gone after a more popular and prestigious career. It happens often in our society. I see people chase the popularity train, never stopping to ask themselves: is this the right career for me? So much talent is lost this way. People convince themselves that they must go for the most lucrative, most prestigious job whether it's a fit for them or not. Because they possess the intellect and abilities to be financial wizards or computer analysts, they seek out the most reputable, well-known firms to work for, rather than using their talents to do what they love.

There've been days when I didn't know if the work I was doing would ever make a difference. I wondered if it would ever mean anything to anyone other than me. My conscious mind would tell me I was wasting my time; no one cares about this stuff except minorities and women. "You could be doing so many other things, man," is what I would hear. But something inside me wouldn't let me quit. I couldn't let stop pursuing diversity. I was hopelessly committed to it. I felt like I had something to offer to the world, and I wanted to share it.

Diversity has always been more than a subject of learning, for me: it's been my life. It opened my eyes to empathy and allowed me to smash through the mental roadblocks, which keeps people from pursuing their dreams. Once I took the oath to allow my subconscious mind to guide me to where I needed to go, I married diversity without a prenuptial agreement. I was all in and couldn't let it go. I took a chance on her and we've lived happily ever since.

It wasn't like I'd never quit anything before. I quit the SWAT team when I was with the State Police and stopped pledging to a fraternity when I was in college. I accept that those things weren't right for me, or I wasn't right for them. I'm an introvert by nature and don't like to hurt people unless I have to. These aren't the best attributes suited for either one. I couldn't break down someone's door on a drug raid then give them a hug afterwards. I couldn't join a fraternity and not want to be around large groups of people.

My introversion and compassion may not have worked in certain instances, but when it came to mastering the art of diversity, they've been strengths for me. As an introvert, I observe and analyze everything. It allows me to see the weaknesses in the way diversity has been presented. Most importantly, I've been able to discover the strengths about the concept, and use them to assist organizations around the globe. Any day that I have the opportunity to teach is a great day, even when people get upset with me and reject what I have to say.

Because I enjoy what I do so much, I'm willing to take it, when it occurs. I'll go the extra mile to ensure that I'm always ready in mind, body, and spirit. I exercise five days a week to make sure my cardiovascular endurance is maintained. Unfortunately, having complete knee replacement surgery has kept me from running, lately, but I walk three to four miles each day and try to talk the entire time. This helps keep my lungs and diaphragm strong during presentations. This allows me to manipulate my vocal cords to emphasis certain phrases or words. It also helps to keep my heart rate down so that my voice doesn't quiver when I get exhausted. Much like singing, it's not only the words that make a hit a song - the delivery is equally important.

## Mentorship, the Fuel for Diversity

Staying committed to learning diversity afforded me the time and experience it takes to become a master of my art, but I didn't do it alone. You'll never hear any bragging from me about being self-made. I had help; help from people who, in most cases, didn't look like me. They didn't come from my neighborhood and didn't share my life experiences. I couldn't tell whether they saw diversity the way I did, but what was clear is that they were more interested in my abilities than what I looked like. There were never any formal agreements made with them to mentor me: it just happened.

My greatest mentor was a White female military officer named Judith Mathewson. I met her at the diversity facilitators training workshop that Dr. Betances, whom I spoke of earlier in the book, was leading. I was lucky enough to have been assigned to her group, and after the first day, she approached me and said: "I need to talk to you about becoming a facilitator in this course!" I excitedly said "sure!" I had no clue what I was getting myself into. Anyone who knows Judy also knows that this woman can talk! If you don't have fast-twitch muscles in your ears, you'll miss about two-thirds of what she's telling you. Judy and I still speak often, but I make sure I do it strategically. I must have a minimum of two hours set aside; phone plugged into a power source and on a long car ride, so that I can talk hands-free. Before knowing better, my arms felt like I'd been lifting weights from holding the phone so long.

But it's all been worth it. When we first met, Judy was a Major in the Air National Guard, assigned to Patrick Air Force Base, Florida. She wasn't my boss, wasn't in my chain of command, and was never stationed with me; but she has been responsible for every major award I received throughout my military career, including the Presidential Lifetime Achievement Award, signed by President Barack Obama. She recommended me for every single one, took the time to write the packages for them, and I won every time. Judy would call me every couple of months and go down a checklist of things I needed to do in my career to get promoted. I did everything she told me - at least, what I could catch as she spoke a thousand miles per hour.

She had no formal responsibility for my career, but it didn't matter to her. She even called my unit and talked to my supervisors about all of the potential I had as an officer, and then sent them the award packet she wrote for me. Judy's mentorship ultimately landed me into her former position at the Defense Equal Opportunity Management Institute at Patrick Air Force Base, where I currently work. Everything she did showed me how critical mentorship is to diversity.

Since I had no family members or friends who were officers to show me the way, I could've easily shortened my career by not attending certain training courses or volunteering for special assignments. These are important opportunities to get noticed by senior officers. Dr. Judith Mathewson, as she is known now, never gave me a handout. She just put her hand out, took me under her wing, and led me through an unfamiliar path. The term "mentor" is derived from the Greek tale *Homer's Odyssey* in which Odysseus, the King of Ithaca, entrusts the care and guidance of his young son Telemachus to his confidant Mentor. Over the centuries, "mentor" has come to be known as a trusted advisor who imparts wisdom and knowledge onto the pupil. If Judy had simply given me professional advice once or twice, I would be more than happy to call her my mentor; but in my case, it wouldn't be an accurate description of her. Therefore, I call her my friend.

Judy has been my most influential mentor, but she wasn't the only one. Johnny Beckwith, my former supervisor at the Defense Equal Opportunity Military Institute, was one of my most important mentors. He was responsible for putting me in charge of the institute's Senior Leadership External Training Branch, which took me around the world, teaching diversity. He chose me based on pure skills and abilities and threw bureaucracy out the window. The position belonged to the Army and I was a member of the Air National Guard. Under normal circumstances, if a position belongs to one organization, it's hardly ever given to another organization to control; especially from Army to Air Force. The Air Force used to fall under the Army's control until 1947, when it was authorized to become an independent branch of service. The Army never forgave us for the divorce. I'm picking on our brothers and sisters in arms. It's part of the military culture to poke fun at each other when the opportunity presents itself. I'm sure if any of them reads this, they'll figure out a way to return the favor.

As it goes, it's rare to have someone put a member of the Air National Guard into such an important assignment. The position serves the entire Department of Defense, teaching diversity and human relations to our senior-ranking military leaders and civilian executive employees. Before placing me in the position, Johnny called me into his office to express his vision for our training directorate. It was different from any meeting I've had with a supervisor. Without my knowledge, he'd been watching my performance the entire time he was there, and he wanted to know more about my experience and abilities. Up to this point in my careers, no one had ever asked me, "What can you bring to the table?"

In the military and in law enforcement, nearly all responsibilities and authority to make decisions are dictated by rank or title. If you don't have much of either, you have little to no authority to do anything besides take care of yourself and follow orders. You can have the greatest ideas known to mankind, and no one cares. "Just do your job!" That's the motto. Not Johnny. He wanted optimal performance by any means necessary, even if it meant putting a weekend warrior in charge. People in the National Guard are often referred to this way because, traditionally, we serve the military part-time and report for duty once a month, on the weekends.

What most people on active duty don't realize is that members of the Guard have multiple skill sets and advanced training, which often exceeds the rank or title they hold in the military. This was certainly the case for me. By the time I landed at DEOMI, I'd spent twenty-plus years as a State Trooper, served as their Equal Employment Compliance Officer, taught diversity for thirteen years, and ran my own diversity consulting business. Had Johnny not taken the time to get to know who I was as a person none of my experiences or skills would've ever been utilized to accomplish our mission. Like the analogy I gave earlier, comparing a cellular phone to diversity, he figured out how to utilize all of my apps.

The lesson for me in all of this was to always take time to get to know your people and never be afraid to take calculated risks when it comes to talent. Asking a person "What can you do?" rather than who are you?" is the beginning of creating diversity. If the person has the skills and ability to perform, who cares what they look like? That's assuming you're looking for commitment to the organization and not simply compliance with orders. Anyone can fill a position: the question is, are they the best person for the job?

People like Judy and Johnny are the difference between an organization just surviving and getting the job done, or thriving and becoming the standard for everyone else. They looked for talent first because they believed in the vision of the organization. For them, it was about getting the best person for the job and recognizing abilities regardless of demographics or some made-up selection process that has nothing to do with performance. Ultimately, if we aren't talking about performance as the driver of diversity, then we're not talking about diversity at all.

Work, the real reason we need diversity, doesn't depend on race, color, gender, or any other category we've created to describe people. Work is dictated by our life and work experiences, and the ability to optimize those experiences to perform well. This is what mentorship has taught me and it's why I'm committed to the concept: "Representation + Inclusion + Performance = Diversity."

## **Diversity Enhanced my Careers**

As a former law enforcement officer, I can attest that policing is one of the most stressful and dangerous jobs one could ever have. You never know what will happen from one day to the next, but you always have to be ready for the worst. It takes a split second to be run over during a traffic stop or to be assaulted by someone high on narcotics. Unless you're conducting a stop on a known violent suspect, officers are trained to keep their weapons holstered during encounters with citizens. You must know the art of persuasion, as discussed earlier, in order to control the situation and get suspects to do what you want them to. Your life can be measured in seconds if you misjudge who is friend or foe. Every person taking the oath to become an officer understands this is the nature of the profession. You deal with people sometimes who hate the institution you represent, and who wouldn't throw a pot of piss on you if you were on fire.

Race and color are at the epicenter of law enforcement, but in different ways then the public may think. As an officer, you're expected to think "Blue" at all times, meaning the culture of law enforcement comes before anything else. If you're African-American, Hispanic, Asian, or female, none of it matters. You think "cop" first! It's the only way to be fully trusted and accepted by your peers.

The saving grace for me was that after the job was over, I could take off my uniform, hang it in my locker, and walk away from the drama. On the flip side, I could never walk away from my blackness; it followed me wherever I went. There was no slipping it off and tucking it away whenever it made people uncomfortable. I never assimilated, and didn't think I needed to. I knew from discovering diversity that the color of my skin would never change anyone's opinion of me, but my performance would. I was able to live in both worlds and have dual perspectives on the job I was doing. It made me a more effective communicator when things hit the fan. If I came upon a situation in which people were ready to throw blows at each other, I was able to bring calm to the situation by speaking their language. Whether in the hood or trailer park, classroom or the boardroom, I could relate. I didn't patronize anyone. I concentrated on what they needed from me as an officer who was trying to help them resolve an issue. This allowed me to listen to what someone was really saying to me, which is critical to effective communication. I'm not the largest person in the world, so effective communication was key to getting the job done without having to get physical with people.

The empathy I learned during my search for true diversity allowed me to take into consideration the circumstances that led to people taking drugs, becoming alcoholics, stealing, robbing, or even murdering someone. I didn't have to agree with it or approve of anyone's lifestyle, but I could understand the causes. If the causes of a situation aren't addressed, it's hard to effectively administer the law. As an officer, arresting the same people every weekend is frustrating. It can feel like the justice system doesn't match the efforts put out to catch some of these folks. Jumping over fences, chasing people through pit bull-lined back yards, losing a boot in the swamp, or getting blood on you from someone who may have HIV or Hepatitis C is scary as hell. After experiencing all of that, to see the person you went through all that hell to catch walking the streets the next day or within a few hours, is demoralizing.

However, the patience I developed over the years of teaching diversity translated well during hostile encounters.

At times, I'd let people vent while I stood there completely silent and expressionless. Eventually they'd calm down enough to listen. Once they settled down, I was able to explain why they were being pulled over or questioned. It made my job much easier and everyone got home, or off to jail, safely.

Law Enforcement and teaching diversity are similar in that the quality of performance rests on an ability to communicate effectively. The art of persuasion is also an essential element for both careers. As a diversity practitioner, it takes persuasion to get participants to buy in to your message; but as a cop, you need it to stay alive. I've been fortunate to accomplish both. Today, when I tell people I'm a retired police officer, they take the liberty of asking my opinion about controversial issues such as the murders of unarmed African-American men killed by police or the retaliatory murders of police officers in Dallas and Baton Rouge that followed. When I express sorrow for the officers being murdered, then follow up with an explanation of the frustration and fear that African-Americans and other minorities have concerning the entire legal system in America. People look at me as if to say, "You are supposed to pick a side!"

Some feel that I should (or would) be pro-cop, and state: "But you were a cop; doesn't it make you angry that people are murdering fellow officers?" Of course I am! I'm upset and afraid for what officers have to experience on a daily basis; most of who never abuse their powers or pull their weapons on anyone. I've been to funerals for officers who've lost their lives in the line of duty; it's tough seeing their families distraught over their sudden death. However, when I express the same remorse from seeing people who look like me being gunned down for reasons that didn't rise to the level of an arrest, the reaction from those asking my opinion is drastically different.

It was as though I was supposed to disregard the fact that I'm also an African-American who has African-American sons, brothers, uncles, and a father; all of whom could easily be the victims of the cultural fears held by some of the officers in these cases. It didn't seem to be enough reason for my dual sympathy, in this case. Judging by their facial expressions, they seemed conflicted when I stated: "I'm not sure that being an ex-cop would erase my anger and lifetime of pain if any of them were to be shot and killed while they were unarmed and posed no threat." In either case, I'm proud to have been a law enforcement officer, and would never apologize for being one. However, I also love who I am as an African-American, and wouldn't want to be anything else. I don't need to be "pro" one or the other to have love for both. I'm able to embrace this dual-cultural experience as a result of learning the concept of diversity. It's given me the opportunity to see the world from different perspectives simultaneously.

Being at the intersection of such profound social issues inspired me to focus on how to improve human relations. There are times when picking a side is less important than making the world a better place to live.

My experience with diversity in the military has also given me opportunities that I never would've imagined. It's given me the opportunity to support my country in my own unique way. I get the chance to speak to our troops about the importance of teamwork, using my passion for diversity to do so. I've traveled around the globe to places like Germany, Riyadh, Jeddah, and Bahrain, providing equal opportunity and diversity training to our troops deployed abroad. I would've never thought a position like this existed in the military, let alone anticipated being in charge of it. Every trip has opened my eyes to a vast array of cultures and beliefs, shedding new light on human nature. Traveling abroad woke me up to different perspectives on how the rest of the world views America. People debate whether we actually have a culture specific to our country. The fabric of the United States is created from so many different cultural influences that it can't be described in a homogenous way. Ethnicity, which is more responsible for our beliefs and practices, is completely left out of the conversation. For that reason alone, "culture," for Americans, is difficult to define.

Some foreigners view us as patriotic people who are kind and generous while others see us as downright evil and represent greed and oppression. It's safe to say we have people who fit both sides of the debate. However, whenever I travel abroad, I love to counter the negative perceptions, especially about people of color. It's an opportunity to dispel some of the myths about who Americans are as a nation, and who I am as a man of color. I've sat with locals in their country where conversations went like this: "You aren't like the Americans I've heard about." "Really! How?" "You aren't arrogant and don't treat me like I'm beneath you." I know that the way I treat people has a great deal to do with my own experiences with racism. These include being called a nigger during a football game, being followed relentlessly through stores to make sure I wasn't stealing, or (once) having a woman I arrested for drunk driving refuse to get in the car with me alone because, as she put it: "You're a black man; you might attack me!"

These experiences didn't break me because diversity taught me who I was as a person and what I could do. I used them as mental workouts to make me stronger and more resilient. I value my unique life experiences more than ever, and learned how to take advantage of the opportunities presented to me. I recognize my strengths and use them accordingly. At this stage of my life, I don't concern myself with my weaknesses. I try to stay away from the things that expose them and capitalize on what I do well. I'm not sure how much time I have on this earth, so I want to get everything out of life that I can.

Diversity enhanced my life in that it took me out of my comfort zone and forced me to engage with people from all walks of life. It made me a better communicator because I had to listen. Listening is critical to effective communication, and I got a lot of practice. In my police capacity, I'd listen to a drug dealer or murderer; as a consultant, I'd listen to a business owner who wants to improve employee productivity. As a Military Equal Opportunity Officer, I'd listen to a military commander concerned about a discrimination complaint all in the same week. What I learned from listening is that they all wanted the same thing: to be effective at what they did. The language they used to express it, the way they approached problems, or the manner in which they chose to make decisions may have appeared to be different; but they really weren't. Only the circumstances they faced were dissimilar. Listening to so many diverse groups can show the commonalities we have as people. If we take a few minutes to listen to each other, we'll find common characteristics that will enable us to work more efficiently and effectively together.

Through it all, I was able to keep my personal integrity and, at the same time, allow others to keep theirs. Discovering diversity made this possible by forcing me to focus on my qualities and skills rather than my physical traits. Until this reversal of thought is established, it's difficult to appreciate the concept. It's also difficult to maximize performance because appearance can be a barrier to success, if you allow it. You can get stuck, waiting on society to approve your body type or hairstyle just to be considered acceptable. After a while, you can chase the status quo to the point that you no longer know who you are. Diversity allows you to be yourself. There are no prerequisites. Be the hell-raising "whatever" you want to be!

## The Gift that Keeps Giving

A few years ago, I taught a diversity course to some senior military leaders, and a middle-aged African-American female asked: "Mr. Richardson how did you fight through all the obstacles to get to where you are today?" It wasn't the first time I'd been asked, but everything about the way she presented the question gave me reason to believe she wanted the key to overcoming racism, discrimination and hatred. It was in the tone of her voice. It carried an octave that only a struggling heart could make; one that has been through the trials and tribulations of trying to make it. It's a rejection thing. If it's happened to you, it's easy to recognize when you hear it.

Before, when asked, I'd explain the mechanics of how I overcame obstacles like worrying about how people saw me, or whether they liked me or not, and how I blocked self-doubt from impeding my journey. This woman didn't need a speech on inner strength - she already had that. What she was asking for was the key - the key that allows one to excel at being themselves while working in an environment where they'll never be the majority and never have power. Her question required a real answer, an experience. I couldn't bullshit her with some statement urging her to just keep working hard and one day it would happen. Too many people had tried that method, only to be derailed by the gatekeepers of acceptance in the workplace - those who only want to see their kind succeed. I decided to tell her about a debt I owed to someone for giving me an opportunity. It was the only way I could be authentic and give her what she was looking for.

It was during 9/11, and I was employed as both a New York State Trooper and a member of the New York Air National Guard. Both are state jobs, which made the governor of the state at that time, George Pataki, my boss on both sides. A month before the tragedy, I was in the middle of completing my processing to become an officer in the Air National Guard. You had to have received a commission by age thirty-five, and I was thirty-four when the planes struck the towers. I couldn't continue my processing because of the magnitude of the emergency. The governor exempted military duties for Guard members who were also State Troopers and hadn't been federally activated for military service. The state needed us to serve in our law enforcement capacity to augment the NYPD's efforts to secure the city. Unfortunately, our services in NYC came to an end on Feb 10. I turned thirty-five on Feb 5th; too old to receive a commission.

I could've easily explained my issue to the governor's office and I'm sure they probably would've made an exception, but that wouldn't have looked good on my behalf. No commander wants their boss to be presented an issue before he or she does, so I went to everyone I could think of in my unit, for help. One by one, they all told me they couldn't help me. I must've asked everyone from the custodians to the landscaping crew. I knew I was capable; not because I was black, not because I was a man, but because I was confident in my abilities. I wasn't going to give up on one of my dreams, so I went to the boss, the Base Commander. He was a tall, lean White guy whose presence was felt in any room he stepped in. With squared shoulders, salt and pepper hair, and piercing blue eyes, he looked like a leader. Normally, I'd save the lessons learned for last; but in this case, it's fitting right here. What I'm about to tell you next is the reason why you should never stop pursuing your dreams. You never know how many gifts you'll receive on your journey.

The day I went to see the commander wasn't the first time we'd met. Two years prior, I was sitting in a U-turn on patrol when over the hill came a shiny red Porsche traveling over the speed limit. New Yorkers assume that traffic signs are merely suggestions and not laws. I pulled out of the U-Turn and was able to catch up with the vehicle. As I approached, I could see the driver was wearing a military flight suit. I thought to myself, "Should I give this guy a ticket or counsel him and let him go?" "Sir! Do you know why I'm stopping you today?"

"Yes trooper, I was going a little fast." No arguing, no sarcasm - just plain honesty. I decided to give him a word of caution instead of a reprimand. Something told me it was the best thing to do. Boy was I right! I had no idea that, two years later, this would be the person that would hold my fate in his hands. He was now the man, Número Uno, the boss; and now I'd get the chance to ask him for help. It was like a scene from the movie "Godfather" and I was going to see Don

Corleone for a favor. I was praying he'd remember me from the traffic stop two years prior. I set up an appointment to see him and, thank God, he remembered me. It probably helped that I introduced myself as Trooper Richardson the guy who'd stopped him on the interstate two years ago when he was driving his red Porsche a bit too fast! That entire statement was my name that day. I needed to make sure he knew exactly who I was and remembered how I'd used my abilities to make sound judgments - just the kind of qualities one needs, to become an officer.

I explained to him that I wasn't able to complete my officer candidate processing due to my obligation to the state as a trooper during 9/11. He looked me straight in the eyes and said, "Gary, you can get anything in this world if you know how to ask and who to ask. I got you covered. I will give you an age waiver so you can continue your processing." Hot damn! Is this real life? If he'd told me he couldn't help me, he would've been doing his job. He could've said "Sorry, those are the rules," and I'd have had to accept it. Instead, he used his authority to grant me an opportunity. With this one act, he incorporated Affirmative Action, equal employment opportunity, and diversity. I don't believe he deliberately set out to check all these boxes, but he did what he felt was the best for the organization and me.

Retired Maj.General Robert K. Knuaff not only changed my life, but also helped steer the path to success for generations of Richardson's to come. By helping me fulfill one dream of being a commissioned officer in the military, it led to me being selected as a commissioned officer within the State Police. The training and experience I received, as a Military Equal Opportunity Officer was second to none. When I interviewed for the Equal Employment Compliance

Officer position with the State Police, I stood out among the rest. There wasn't a question I couldn't answer, and I was able to provide additional information concerning equal employment opportunity that the review board wasn't privy to.

Both positions were promotions, which put me in a higher tax bracket. This allowed me to send my youngest son to one of the best private schools in New York State. Now he's going into his third year in college and doing very well for himself. None of this would've happened without the General giving me an opportunity. I did my part to prepare myself. I knew Affirmative Action was and still is needed to create opportunities for women and minorities, but I wasn't going to depend on it. That still gives too much power to someone else. I wanted to be so good they couldn't ignore me. I believe that's what the General saw in my eyes.

"Ma'am, this is why, in spite of all the negativity and discrimination I've experienced along the way, I kept grinding. I felt that everything I went through was preparing me for something. Just what, I didn't know; but something. That 'something' turned out to be diversity. It's not just a subject I teach - it's a way of life for me. I've found my purpose. It's more important to me than any obstacle racism or discrimination has presented. That's how I made it to this point."

Once I finished telling her my story, she sat silent for a few minutes, reflecting on what I said. Maybe she had a similar experience in her life that may have gotten overshadowed by disappointments in the workplace. Maybe she just needed a moment to process what I revealed. After a pause, she looked up at me and with a tremble in her voice, she said: "Thank you so much for sharing that with me."

Telling her about my experience forged an even deeper understanding of diversity for me. As I was reliving the events that led me to being in the position to answer her question, I realized that diversity has almost nothing to do with race, color, sex, or any other demographic category we've come up with.

I say 'almost nothing' because we've made these things count in order to segregate people and groups within our society. If it weren't for that, diversity as we know it would be strictly about performance and nothing else. We wouldn't need to keep count of how many women or minorities we had in the workplace - they would've already been there. We wouldn't need to create new bathroom areas to accommodate women in fire departments or military units - they would've already been built. There'd be no special recruiting drives needed to find qualified minorities. Recruiting would only serve to find people with the talent and capabilities to perform the job - what it's intended for in the first place. If we could get to the point of hiring in spite of demographics, as a country we wouldn't need Affirmative Action, Equal Employment Opportunity, or demographic diversity. These things would happen naturally, without the need for terms like these.

If diversity is something an organization wants to improve upon, the focus should be placed on the positive opportunities it brings. This is why I addressed the woman's question the way I did and spared her the details of my fight against discrimination and racism. It's the same reason I didn't give them the spotlight in this book. Diversity is about moving forward, not backward. She wanted to know how I was able to succeed. The truth is, I turned every negative situation into a positive. When I was met with discrimination,

I fought strategically at times and tactically at others. If I had a goal which required a longer period of time to develop, I fought strategically, passing on the opportunity to address the racism I experienced. I had to stick around long enough to see my plan through to fruition so I could become the shot-caller. Then I could cut the disease of racism completely out of my environment. On other occasions, I responded immediately to let people know who I was and where I stood. If the negativity was coming from a peer trying to assert some sort of power over me, it had to be dealt with quickly, or else it would never stop. In either case, I made sure to get something positive out of it.

When creating diversity initiatives, I urge leaders to use negative experiences they've encountered along the way as lessons learned, not as reasons to give up and discard their efforts. There will always be opposition against including people who don't fit the mold of what some call "normal". Normalcy is predictable: it means having a consistent pattern of behavior whether it benefits you or not. You can't be normal and embrace diversity at the same time. It's like mixing oil and water. Both are important and have their purpose, but they don't work well together. Be a great leader and take some risks. The worst you can get by being an inclusive leader is to find out which employees are good performers and which aren't!

The current human relations climate in America has confirmed two things for me: A true understanding of diversity is more important now than ever and we are going through a cultural revolution, which is frightening to many people. Some welcome the changes we've experienced with same sex marriage, immigration, and civil rights for those who are transgender, while others view these steps as attacks on the American way of life. I don't have the answer for what's right or wrong, but I'm an optimist, I don't see America's greatness eroding away. We're just going through some labor pains and developing a few stretch marks from the fetus whose name is "Tolerance."

*Diversity isn't a political, religious, White, black, female or male, bisexual, gay or transgender thing. It's an active process created as a mechanism to enable diverse groups of people to work together efficiently and effectively. Diversity in the workplace requires leadership that's willing to sacrifice some personal beliefs and stereotypes about culture for the sake of optimal performance. At the end of the day, performance is what truly matters. If it's not Representation + Inclusion + Performance working together as one, it's not diversity.*

## NOTES

Pg. 9 http://www.catalyst.org/knowledge/women-CEOs-sp-500

Pg. 19 http://www.bbc.com/news/world-us-Canada-36020717

Pg. 38 FUBU was an urban clothing line created in the 90's by an African American entrepreneur named Daymond John

Pg. 70 Laura Liswood discusses her experience with diversity as a senior advisor for Goldman Sachs

Pg. 80 Saul McLeod, "Maslow's Hierarchy of Needs" www.simplypsychology.org/maslow.html#needs5 2014

Pg. 81 Kendra Sherry is a psychological expert who writes for About.com on Maslow's Theory of Needs in the article "What is Self-Actualization," dated December 17, 2015.

Pg. 84 Green, Daryl. *Mastery*.

Pg. 91 (https://www.uky.edu/-eushe2/Pajares/OnFailingG.html)

Pg. 103 http://www.rollingstone.com/music/artists/jimi_hendrix/biography

Pg. 133 Neilson Report 2015, http://www.nielsen.com/content/dam/corporate/us/en/reports downloads/2015-reports/african-american-consumer-untold-story-sept-2015.pdf

Pg. 133 downloades/ 2015 african-american-consumer-untold-story-sept-2015.pdf

## ABOUT THE AUTHOR

Mr. Gary Richardson has traveled the globe teaching senior level military leaders and civilians about the advantages of having diverse workforces and how to tap into the hidden potential of all employees. He has a long and distinguished career as an officer in the military and is a proud retiree of the New York State Police. Mr. Richardson is a highly decorated equal opportunity and diversity expert who's dedicated his life to helping organizations get the best out of its employees and service members. He resides in Florida and continues his quest to bring clarity on the topic of diversity.

Made in the USA
Middletown, DE
23 July 2019